UNION
WITH CHRIST

UNION
WITH CHRIST

IN SCRIPTURE, HISTORY, AND THEOLOGY

Robert Letham

PUBLISHING

P.O. BOX 817 • PHILLIPSBURG • NEW JERSEY 08865-0817

Page design and typesetting by Lakeside Design Plus

Printed in the United States of America

Library of Congress Cataloging-in-Publication Data

Letham, Robert.
  Union with Christ : in Scripture, history, and theology / Robert Letham.
    p. cm.
  Includes bibliographical references (p.   ) and indexes.
  ISBN 978-1-59638-063-9 (pbk.)
  1. Mystical union. 2. Jesus Christ--Person and offices. 3. Reformed Church--Doctrines.
I. Title.

  BT767.7.L48 2011
  232'.8--dc23

                                        2011016916

For Joan

Elizabeth and Christopher

Caroline and Leo, and Levi

Adam

Contents

Acknowledgments   ix

Abbreviations   xi

Introduction   1

1. Creation   9

2. Incarnation   19

3. Pentecost   45

4. Union with Christ and Representation   57

5. Union with Christ and Transformation   85

6. Union with Christ in Death and Resurrection   129

Bibliography   143

Index of Scripture   153

Index of Subjects and Names   159

Acknowledgments

Those who have read my earlier book *The Work of Christ* (Leicester, UK: Inter-Varsity Press; Downers Grove, IL: InterVarsity Press, 1993) will be aware that union with Christ is a theme in which I have had an interest for some time. In that book I devoted a chapter to it. Who could fail to be interested in something that lies right at the heart of biblical soteriology? This present volume represents the distillation of thought over a range of areas down the years. It makes it more than difficult to do full justice to all the influences that may have impinged on me in that time. It reminds us that it is extremely hazardous to posit specific influences on particular authors without tangible evidence to support such claims.

So let me confine myself to more immediate indebtedness. I am very thankful to Dr. Richard B. Gaffin Jr., Professor of Biblical and Systematic Theology Emeritus, Westminster Theological Seminary, Philadelphia, and Dr. William B. Evans, Younts Professor of Bible and Religion, Erskine College, Due West, South Carolina, for reading through the draft chapters and making very useful suggestions. Neither can be charged with any errors or misconceptions in this book, which are entirely my own, nor with the views expressed in it. Dr. Michael Horton, J. Gresham Machen Professor of Systematic Theology and Apologetics, Westminster Seminary California, Escondido, California, also took a look at one draft section and saved me a lot of anguish by his comments, insofar as I determined to omit the section and return to it on another occasion.

On the bibliographical front, my thanks are due to the Rev. Peter H. Lewis of Nottingham for recommending that I consult the seventeenth-century Puritan author Rowland Stedman, who wrote a significant treatise on the subject. Dr. Mark Garcia pointed me to the correspondence between John Calvin and Pietro Martire Vermigli in 1555; this was before his own important work was published. I have benefited from the services of the British

Library and also Cambridge University Library, especially the Rare Books Room. Once again, Early English Books Online has been a great resource.

Special appreciation is due, as usual, to those at P&R Publishing who have helped in the preparation of this book. Marvin Padgett, Vice President, Editorial, has encouraged me on an ongoing basis, while thanks are also due to Barbara Lerch and Jeremy Kappes. John J. Hughes and Karen Magnuson have been an extremely perceptive and assiduous editorial team.

I am thankful for the faculty, staff, and students of Wales Evangelical School of Theology, where I teach. Even more so, I am grateful to my wife, Joan, for her constant and loving support.

Above all, I give thanks to the God we worship—the Father, the Son, and the Holy Spirit in the unity of their indivisible being—for granting us union with Christ, so making us partakers of the divine nature, of which, as Calvin wrote, "nothing more outstanding can be imagined."

Abbreviations

BDAG	Walter Bauer, Frederick William Danker, William Arndt, and F. Wilbur Gingrich, eds., *A Greek-English Lexicon of the New Testament and Other Early Christian Literature*, 3rd ed. (Chicago: University of Chicago Press, 2001)
BQ	*Baptist Quarterly*
CD	Karl Barth, *Church Dogmatics*, ed. Geoffrey W. Bromiley and Thomas F. Torrance, 4 vols. (Edinburgh: T&T Clark, 1956–77)
CO	John Calvin, *Opera quae supersunt omnia*, ed. Guilielmus Baum, Eduardus Cunitz, and Eduardus Reiss, 59 vols., *Corpus Reformatorum*, vols. 29–87 (Brunswick: C. A. Schwetschke and Son, 1863–1900)
CTJ	*Calvin Theological Journal*
EQ	*Evangelical Quarterly*
ESV	English Standard Version
Institutes	John Calvin, *Institutes of the Christian Religion*, ed. Ford Lewis Battles and John T. McNeill (1559; repr., Philadelphia: Westminster Press, 1960)
JETS	*Journal of the Evangelical Theological Society*
LN	Johannes P. Louw and Eugene A. Nida, eds., *Greek-English Lexicon of the New Testament Based on Semantic Domains* (New York: United Bible Societies, 1988)
LS	Henry George Liddell and Robert Scott, *A Greek-English Lexicon*, rev. Henry Stuart Jones, 9th ed. (Oxford: Clarendon Press, 1940)
NT	New Testament

OS	*Joannis Calvini Opera Selecta*, ed. Petrus Barth and Guilelmus Niesel, 5 vols. (Munich: Christoph Kaiser, 1926–52)
OT	Old Testament
PG	J. P. Migne et al., eds., *Patrologia graeca* (Paris, 1857–66)
PL	J. P. Migne et al., eds., *Patrologia Latina* (Paris, 1878–90)
SBET	*Scottish Bulletin of Evangelical Theology*
SCJ	*Sixteenth Century Journal*
SJT	*Scottish Journal of Theology*
ST	Thomas Aquinas, *Summa Theologica*
SW	*Selected Works of John Calvin: Tracts and Letters*, ed. Henry Beveridge and Jules Bonnet, 7 vols. (1858; repr., Grand Rapids: Baker, 1987)
WCF	Westminster Confession of Faith
Wing	Donald Wing, *Short-Title Catalogue of Books Printed in England, Scotland, Ireland, Wales and British America, and of English Books Printed in Other Countries, 1641–1700* (New York: Index South, 1945)
WLC	Westminster Larger Catechism
WSC	Westminster Shorter Catechism
WTJ	*Westminster Theological Journal*

Introduction

Union with Christ is right at the center of the Christian doctrine of salvation. The whole of our relationship with God can be summed up in such terms. John Calvin agreed when he wrote: "For we await salvation from him not because he appears to us afar off, but because he makes us, ingrafted into his body, participants not only in all his benefits but also in himself."[1] WLC 65–90 describes our entire salvation as union and communion with Christ in grace and glory. John Murray considered that "nothing is more central or basic than union and communion with Christ,"[2] for it "is the central truth of the whole doctrine of salvation."[3] In the words of Lane Tipton, "there are no benefits of the gospel apart from union with Christ."[4]

The task of understanding what this means is made a lot harder by the limits of our human finitude. The literature discusses at some length the relationship between union with Christ and justification, sanctification, or some other such matter. When one asks what in fact this union consists in, however, what it actually *is*, there is a general silence. It is not difficult to see why this is so. The reality far surpasses the ability of human language to describe it. Being united to Christ involves union with the Son of God, who himself transcends our finitude. Being indwelt by the Holy Spirit entails union with the whole Trinity. This goes beyond what we can even imagine.

Yet the fact of the incarnation should be enough to alert us to the truth that we have been made by God to be compatible with him. If we cannot reach up to God to penetrate the divine mysteries, he has reached down to reveal himself truly and faithfully to us in Christ his Son. He has left a written record in Scripture. We are not left to grope in the dark in blissful ignorance.

---

1. *Institutes*, 3.2.24.
2. John Murray, *Redemption Accomplished and Applied* (London: Banner of Truth, 1961), 161.
3. Ibid., 170.
4. Lane G. Tipton, "Union with Christ and Justification," in *Justified in Christ: God's Plan for Us in Justification*, ed. K. Scott Oliphint (Fearn, Ross-shire, UK: Mentor, 2007), 34.

1

From the middle of the seventeenth century on, however, this great jewel in the crown of God's grace has gone into eclipse. Today not much is said about union with Christ from the pulpit, and until recently, little was written about it. William B. Evans has charted its demise in American Reformed theology. Jonathan Edwards and Charles Hodge, two great stalwarts of the American Reformed tradition, were particularly responsible, he claims, for a division between two aspects of union with Christ that Calvin had held together: the external element of imputation and the transformative element of the work of the Holy Spirit. A tension developed between the desire to maintain the utter graciousness of our salvation, achieved by Christ, applied by the Spirit, received by us—seen particularly in justification only by faith—and, on the other hand, the ongoing work of the Holy Spirit, sent by the Father to indwell us and change us into his image. These two elements were detached and considered in isolation.[5]

Questions have arisen over the relationship between justification and sanctification in Calvin as aspects of union with Christ. I do not have time to discuss this in any detail. Among neoorthodox scholars, it is held that the later Reformed scholastics, in prioritizing justification, departed from Calvin, who dealt with sanctification first in book 3 of the 1559 edition of the *Institutes*. This misses the seismic shift in Reformation and post-Reformation studies associated with Richard Muller and others. Muller has convincingly argued that Calvin, in his *Institutes*, follows the order of teaching in Paul's Letter to the Romans, which provided the basis for his ordering of topics from the 1539 edition onward, largely following Philipp Melanchthon.[6] In doing this, Calvin does not imply by the order of his treatment of topics in book 3 any particular set of priorities in his theology. The idea of an *ordo salutis* was not a live issue at the time Calvin wrote, and it is misleading to search for one in his writings.[7] As I have argued elsewhere, the Westminster Assembly (1643–49) did not discuss a rigorous logical order. It spent most of the time in theological debate related to the exegesis of biblical passages. Topics were discussed on a first-come,

5. William B. Evans, *Imputation and Impartation: Union with Christ in American Reformed Theology* (Eugene, OR: Wipf & Stock, 2008), esp. 111–12.

6. Richard A. Muller, *The Unaccommodated Calvin: Studies in the Foundation of a Theological Tradition* (New York: Oxford University Press, 2000), 118–39.

7. As Muller notes, "The order of *loci* identified by Melanchthon in Paul's Epistle to the Romans thus established a standard for the organization of Protestant theology." Ibid., 129.

first-served basis as the committees presented their respective reports to the full body. Indeed, the idea of a central organizing principle arose only in nineteenth-century German scholarship; it is anachronistic to look for it three hundred years earlier.[8]

Union with Christ cannot be said to control Calvin's soteriology. Still less does it determine the relative order of priority of justification and sanctification in his thought. There is plenty of evidence in the 1559 *Institutes* itself indicating that Calvin shared the views of the later Reformed that justification was foundational. He regards it as "the main hinge on which religion turns," since it is necessary as a foundation on which to establish our salvation and build piety toward God.[9] Yet all this should not lead us to conclude that union with Christ was anything but central and vital to his view of salvation.[10]

From within the ranks of English Puritanism, Rowland Stedman, one of the ministers ejected from their livings in 1662,[11] in an important treatise published in 1668,[12] argued that "in order to an interest in eternal life, and partaking of those blessings which are given forth by Christ . . . it is of absolute necessity, that we be united unto Christ." Therefore, "if we will have life from the Son, we must have the Son; *that is*, we must be made one with him. No union with Jesus, and no communication of life and salvation from Jesus." First the Lord "doth plant them [believers] into Christ, and then bless them in him, and through him."[13]

The Centrality of Union with Christ in the Bible

Union with Christ is crucial to, and at the heart of, the biblical teaching about salvation. In support we can point to a range of significant passages throughout the NT, from a variety of authors.

8. Robert Letham, *The Westminster Assembly: Reading Its Theology in Historical Context* (Phillipsburg, NJ: P&R Publishing, 2009), 101–11, 245–46.
9. *Institutes*, 3.11.1.
10. Ibid., 3.11.6, 11; 3.13.5; see also "Antidote to the Council of Trent," *SW*, 3.128; "Reply to Sadoleto," *SW*, 1.41–42.
11. See *Oxford Dictionary of National Biography*, available at http://www.oxforddnb.com/view /article/26341 (accessed September 23, 2009).
12. Rowland Stedman, *The Mystical Union of Believers with Christ, or A Treatise Wherein That Great Mystery and Priviledge of the Saints Union with the Son of God Is Opened* (London: W. R. for Thomas Parkhurst, at the Golden-Bible on London-Bridge, under the gate, 1668), Wing / 335:13.
13. Ibid., 18.

Paul

In Ephesians 1:3–14, Paul sums up the whole of the Christian faith as entailing union with Christ. From election before the foundation of the world (vv. 3–4), to redemption by the blood of Christ (v. 7), to the earnest of the Holy Spirit, who seals us to the day of redemption (vv. 13–14), all happens *in him, in Christ*, whether it is particularly attributable to the Father, as in election and predestination (vv. 3–5), to the Son in redemption (v. 7), or to the Holy Spirit (vv. 13–14). Indeed, the renovation of the entire cosmos is to occur under the headship of Christ (v. 10).[14]

John

In John 14:16ff., Jesus compares the relationship between his disciples and himself with his own relation to the Father. He and the Father are *in* each other, mutually indwelling in the unity of the Trinity. Moreover, he and the disciples would indwell each other, too. When the Holy Spirit was to come at Pentecost, they would know that "I am in my Father, and you in me, and I in you" (v. 20).

Moreover, Jesus reinforces this concept in what follows. To those who love him and keep his word, "my Father will love him and we will come to him and make our home with him" (v. 23). Here the whole Trinity will take up residence with those who love Jesus and keep his commandments. The Son and the Father will make their home with them, while the context points to the coming of the Spirit as the occasion when this will take place. The word *monē* does not denote a temporary visitation, as when the Spirit came on the prophets; it is a permanent dwelling.[15]

In John 17:21ff., Jesus prays to the Father for his church that it will display a unity before the world in some way analogous to the union the Son has with the Father in the unity of the indivisible Trinity. The Father and the Son are distinct, as is evident in this prayer in which the Son addresses the Father; yet they are one. Their oneness does not erode the distinction, nor does the distinction sever their oneness. In verse 21, he speaks of the unity of the church—"that they may be one"—and the union of the Father and the Son, and makes the latter the template of the former—"just as you, Father, are in me, and I in you, that they also may be in us." From this, those

---

14. Robert Letham, *The Work of Christ* (Leicester, UK: Inter-Varsity Press, 1993), 80–81.
15. D. A. Carson, *The Gospel according to St John* (Leicester, UK: Inter-Varsity Press, 1991), 504–5.

who were to believe in him through the testimony of the apostles would be *in* the Father and the Son.

He adds the prayer "that they may be one even as we are one, *I in them and you in me*, that they may become perfectly one" (vv. 22–23). The unity of believers for which Jesus prays is also grounded in the union the church has with Christ himself. It is clear that the Father and the Son are distinct yet one; their union is a unity-in-distinction. Hence, the unity of believers cannot offset their own particular distinctiveness. Furthermore, it is founded on the fact that the Son is *in* them. Jesus' prayer for his church centers in the fact of his indwelling it and its consequent introduction into the life of God himself.

Peter

In 1 Peter 1:3–4, Peter's introduction shows that he regards the gospel as, at root, focused in union with Christ. The "elect exiles of the dispersion" to whom he writes have been "born again to a living hope through the resurrection of Jesus Christ from the dead." Their regeneration, at the start of their Christian career, occurred through Christ's resurrection. Regeneration is itself a resurrection; Paul wrote of the pre-regenerate state as one of death in sin (Eph. 2:1), with the corollary that regeneration entails a coming to life. In this case, regeneration is sharing in Christ's resurrection and so occurs by the power of that momentous event. It is being made alive with Christ. It does not take place in isolation for this or that person; it is inescapably corporate, in a dynamic union with Christ himself.

Union with Christ and Justification

According to Paul in Romans 5:12–21, just as Adam plunged the whole race into sin and death because of their relationship of solidarity with him, so the second Adam brings life and righteousness to all who sustain a relationship of solidarity with him.

> If, because of one man's trespass, death reigned through that one man, much more will those who receive the abundance of grace and the free gift of righteousness reign in life through the one man Jesus Christ. (Rom. 5:17 ESV)

Here Paul reflects on his previous statement of the one way of salvation from sin by the propitiatory death of Christ, which avails for all who believe

(Rom. 3:21ff.). Justification is received only by faith and is grounded on what Christ did once for all in his death and resurrection (4:25). Paul's point is that we are not addressed merely as discrete individuals; instead, we are placed by God in solidaristic groups or teams. Adam was head or captain of a team of which we all were members. His sin plunged the whole team into sin, ruin, death, and condemnation. What Christ did for us was also done as the head of a team of which we are part. He did it on our behalf, for us—and God reckons it to our account as a result of our being united, through faith, with him as the head of the team. Our justification is therefore grounded on union with Christ.[16]

Union with Christ and Sanctification

In Romans 6:1ff., in answer to charges that his gospel encourages moral indifference, Paul insists that believers, the justified, live to Christ and do not give themselves over to sin. This is because they died with Christ to sin and rose again to new life in his resurrection. Not only did Christ die and rise again *for* them, but they died and rose *with* him. Union with Christ is the foundational basis for sanctification and the dynamic force that empowers it. As Paul says, "Do you not know that as many as were baptized into Christ Jesus were baptized into his death; we were buried with him through baptism into death, so that as Christ was raised from the dead through the glory of the Father so we too should live in newness of life" (6:3–4).

Union with Christ and Resurrection

Paul argues in 1 Corinthians 15 that the resurrection of Christ and the future resurrection of his church is one reality (vv. 12–19). Paul argues back and forth from one to the other. If Christ is not raised, there can be no resurrection of believers. If there is no general resurrection, Christ cannot

---

16. In the last two decades, there has been a huge amount of discussion in NT studies on the relationship between union with Christ and justification. Driven by the New Perspective on Paul, associated particularly with James D. G. Dunn and N. T. Wright but backed up by a host of others, union with Christ is said to render superfluous and mistaken the idea of the imputation of the righteousness of Christ. The literature is too voluminous to cite here. This book does not deal with this issue except tangentially, although I think its argument undermines the New Perspective approach. For an outstanding assessment of this literature from the perspective of Calvin studies and classical Christology, see Mark A. Garcia, "Imputation and the Christology of Union with Christ: Calvin, Osiander and the Contemporary Quest for a Reformed Model," *WTJ* 68 (2006): 219–51.

have been raised himself. The two stand together. In fact, Christ has been raised—and so, therefore, will we be. Christ is the firstfruits of the resurrection of believers at his return (vv. 19–23). Not only is his resurrection first in time, but as firstfruits, it is of the same kind as the full harvest. Hence, it is the guarantee not only that the full harvest will be gathered but that both his resurrection and ours are identical. From this it is clear that the resurrection of believers at the parousia is a resurrection *in Christ*. The resurrections are effectively the same (v. 35ff.). The Einstein-Bell-Podorsky theory of the identical behavior of subatomic particles separated by indefinite space is paralleled here in the resurrection. Christ's resurrection and the resurrection of the righteous, separated by indefinite time, are identical because the latter occurs in union with the former.

As Tony Lane has written, "Until we are united with Christ what he has achieved for us helps us no more than an electricity mains supply that passes our house but is not connected to it."[17]

17. Anthony N. S. Lane, *Justification by Faith in Catholic-Protestant Dialogue: An Evangelical Assessment* (London: T&T Clark, 2002), 23.

O N E

Creation

Union with Christ rests on the basis of the creation of man to be compatible with God. This is at the heart of the message of the first chapter of Genesis, which highlights the creation of man as male and female, and his rule over the created order. So as to see how this relates to our great theme, we will look first at the overall context of the chapter. In summary, it points to God the Creator as a relational being, with man made in his image reflecting this characteristic in himself. Ultimately it points forward to the coming of Jesus Christ, who *is* the image of the invisible God.

The Trinitarian Basis of Creation

The first chapter of Genesis portrays the creation and formation of the world, and the ordered shaping of a place for the human race to live. It presents man as head of creation, in relation to and in communion with God his Creator. The act of *creation* itself is direct and immediate (vv. 1–2), distinct from the work of formation that follows.[1] The result is a cosmos formless, empty, dark, and wet—unfit for human life. The rest of the chapter describes the world's *formation* (or *distinction*) and *adornment*, God's introducing of order, light, and dryness, making it fit for life to flourish. First, God creates light, and sets boundaries to the darkness (vv. 2–5). Second, he molds

1. Herman Bavinck, *In the Beginning: Foundations of Creation Theology*, ed. John Bolt, trans. John Vriend (Grand Rapids: Baker, 1999), 100ff. (subsequently published in volume 2 of Bavinck's *Reformed Dogmatics*). See also the discussion in *ST*, pt. 1a, Q. 66, arts. 1–4, and the entire section QQ. 66–74 in general.

9

the earth into shape so that it is no longer formless (vv. 6–8, 9–10). Third, God separates the waters and forms dry land, so that it is no longer entirely wet (vv. 9–10). Following this, he populates the earth, ending its emptiness (vv. 20–30), first with fish and birds, then with land animals, and finally, as the apex of the whole, with human beings made in his image. This God is not only almighty but also a master planner, artist, and architect supreme. This order is clear from the parallels between two groups of days: the first three and the second three.[2] In all this God shows his sovereign freedom in naming and blessing his creation, and sees it as thoroughly good. At the end comes the unfinished seventh day, when God enters his rest, which he made to share with man, his partner, whom he created in his own image. There is an implicit invitation for us to follow.[3]

Particularly striking is God's sovereign and variegated ordering of his creation. In particular, he forms the earth in a threefold manner. First, he issues direct fiats. He says, "Let there be light," and there is light (v. 3). So, too, he brings into being with seemingly effortless command the expanse (v. 6), the dry ground (v. 9), the stars (vv. 14–15), the birds and the fish (vv. 20–21). Each time it is enough for God to speak, and his edict is fulfilled. Second, he works. He separates the light from the darkness (v. 4), he makes the expanse and separates the waters (v. 7), he makes the two great lights (the sun and the moon) (v. 16), and sets them in the expanse to give light on the earth (v. 17), he creates the great crea-tures of the seas and various kinds of birds (v. 21), he makes the beasts of the earth and reptiles (v. 25), and finally he creates man—male and female—in his own image (vv. 26–27). The thought is of focused, pur-posive action by God, of divine labor accomplishing his ends. But there is also a third way of formation, in which God uses the activity of the creatures themselves. God commands the earth to produce vegetation, plants, and trees (vv. 11–12). He commands the lights to govern the day and night (vv. 14–16). He commands the earth to bring forth land animals (v. 24). Here the creatures follow God's instructions and contribute to the eventual outcome. This God who created the universe does not work in

---

2. This pattern was discerned at least as long ago as the thirteenth century. See *Robert Grosseteste: On the Six Days of Creation: A Translation of the Hexaëmeron*, trans. C. F. J. Martin, Auctores Britan-nici Medii Aevi (Oxford: Oxford University Press for the British Academy, 1996), 160–61 (5:1:3–5:2:1); *ST*, pt. 1, Q. 74, art. 1. See my article "'In the Space of Six Days': The Days of Creation from Origen to the Westminster Assembly," *WTJ* 61 (1999): 149–74.

3. Cf. Heb. 3:7–4:11.

formed of one block

a monolithic way. His order is varied—it is threefold but one. His work shows diversity in its unity and unity in diversity. This God loves order and variety together.[4] — *union or group of 3*

This reflects what the chapter records of God himself. The triadic manner of the earth's formation reflects who God its Creator is. He is a relational being. This is implicit from the very start. We notice a distinction between God who created the heavens and earth (v. 1), the Spirit of God who hovers over the face of the waters (v. 2), and the speech or word of God issuing the fiat "Let there be light" (v. 3). His speech recurs frequently throughout the chapter. While it is most unlikely that the author and original readers would have understood the Spirit of God in a personalized way, because of the heavy and insistent stress in the OT on the uniqueness of the one God, Gordon Wenham is sound when he suggests that this is a vivid image of the Spirit of God.[5] The later NT personalizing of the Spirit of God is a congruent development from this statement.

With the creation of man is the unique deliberation "Let us make man in our image," which expresses a plurality in God (vv. 26–27). Gerhard Von Rad says that this signifies the high point and goal to which all of God's creative activity is directed.[6] Since Scripture has a fullness that goes beyond the horizons of the original authors, the many church fathers who saw this as a reference to the Trinity were on the right track. While this was concealed from the original readers and from the OT saints as a whole, and was not how it was understood then, the fathers were certainly not at variance with the trajectory of the text. Rabbinical commentators were often perplexed by this passage and other similar ones referring to a plurality in God (Gen. 3:22; 11:7; Isa. 6:8). The NT gives us the principle that the OT contains in seed form what is more fully made known in the NT, and on that basis we may look back to the earlier writings, much as at the end of a detective mystery we reread the plot, seeing clues that we missed the first time but are now given fresh meaning by our knowledge of the whole. In terms of the *sensus plenior* (the "fuller meaning") of Scripture, these words of God attest a plurality in God, which later came to be expressed in the doctrine of the Trinity. The original readers would not

---

4. See Francis Watson, *Text, Church, and World: Biblical Interpretation in Theological Perspective* (Edinburgh: T&T Clark, 1994), 142–43.

5. Gordon J. Wenham, *Genesis 1–15*, Word Biblical Commentary (Waco, TX: Word, 1987), 15–17.

6. Gerhard Von Rad, *Genesis: A Commentary*, rev. ed. (Philadelphia: Westminster Press, 1961).

have grasped this, but we, with the full plot disclosed, can revisit the passage and see there the clues.[7]

I have written elsewhere, commenting on Genesis 1:26–27, that "man exists as a duality, the one in relation to the other. . . . As for God himself . . . the context points to his own intrinsic relationality. The plural occurs on three occasions in v. 26, yet God is also singular in v. 27. God is placed in parallel with man, made in his image as male and female, who is described both in the singular and plural. Behind it all is the distinction God/Spirit of God/speech of God in vv. 1–3 . . . This relationality will in the development of biblical revelation eventually be disclosed as taking the form of a triunity."[8] I refer there to kindred comments by Karl Barth.[9]

Christ as Mediator of Creation

Flowing from the biblical presentation of creation as a work of the whole Trinity comes the NT assertion of the creation mediatorship of Jesus Christ. I have discussed this theme elsewhere.[10] It is found in John 1, where the Logos is described as existing "in the beginning," a phrase strongly reminiscent of Genesis 1:1. This Logos, who was with God and who was God, who became flesh and lived among us, is also described as the Creator of all things (John 1:3). This follows from his being life itself; he is not merely the Author of life, as if life were something independent and autonomous, but he himself *is* life (v. 4). His creating is free, but it is also an expression of who he is.

Paul expounds a similar theme in Colossians 1:16–17, where he affirms that "all things were created in him, things in heaven and on earth, things visible and invisible; whether thrones and dominions, rulers and authorities, all things were created through him and to him. And he is before all things, and in him all things hold together." In this Paul argues that Christ as the preexistent Son (cf. v. 13) is the Creator of the universe. "All things" is comprehensive, excluding nothing. Personal and impersonal, angelic and human, animal and plant—all owe their existence to the Son. Moreover, not only did he create them all, but he did so in such a way that he is their head.

---

7. Robert Letham, *The Holy Trinity: In Scripture, History, Theology, and Worship* (Phillipsburg, NJ: P&R Publishing, 2004), 17–22.

8. Robert Letham, "The Man-Woman Debate: Theological Comment," *WTJ* 52 (1990): 71.

9. *CD*, 3.1:196.

10. Robert Letham, *The Work of Christ* (Leicester, UK: Inter-Varsity Press, 1993), 197–209.

Creation was made *in Christ*. In turn, the cosmos has a purpose. It is held together by the Son. He sustains it at every moment and directs it toward the end he intends for it. That end is himself. All things were created and are sustained *for Christ*. The reason the universe exists is for the glory of Christ, the Son of God. The goal toward which it is heading is conformity to him. As Paul wrote to the Ephesians, all things will be under the headship of Christ for eternity (Eph. 1:10).[11]

The author of Hebrews describes the Son in whom God's final word has been given as the One who created the ages (Heb. 1:2) and who continues to uphold all things by his powerful word, directing them to the end he has eternally intended (v. 3). As has been widely noted, the imagery is not static, as if he were carrying the world as a dead weight, but dynamic, directing it purposefully to its destined goal. There is more than a hint here that the author is identifying Christ, the Son, with the word spoken at creation (cf. Gen. 1:3).

Furthermore, in the great vision in Revelation 5, John sees that the Lamb alone is both able and worthy to open the seals and so to govern world affairs. He is sovereign over all that happens in the world and to his church. The rest of the book spells this out in terms of judgment on the world and ultimate victory for the persecuted church.[12]   ·

Man Created in Christ, the Image of God

As we noted, the high point of the chapter is the creation of the first Adam *in* the image of God (Gen. 1:26–27); it is the only place here in which the self-deliberation of God is recorded. It is as though the author were taking a highlighter and marking these statements as absolutely crucial to a grasp of the whole. In short, this is the focus of the chapter, the goal to which it is moving. What does it mean? In the NT, Paul says that believers are being renewed in the image of God in knowledge, righteousness, and holiness (Eph. 4:24; Col. 3:10). The question whether fallen man is still the image of God and, if so, in what sense this is true has been debated at great length through the years. Some statements in the Bible suggest that

11. Ibid., 198–202.
12. See, inter alia, G. K. Beale, *The Book of Revelation: A Commentary on the Greek Text* (Grand Rapids: Eerdmans, 1999).

this is true of all people, regardless of their relationship to God,[13] whereas these Pauline passages imply that it is true only for those renewed by the Holy Spirit. Reformed theologians have understood this dilemma in terms of a dual aspect to man as the image of God, speaking of the image in the broader sense, in which all participate, and in the narrower sense, which relates only to Christian believers. This has appeared unsatisfactory in a range of ways. The resolution is to be found in terms of redemptive history. In doing so, we are retrieving what the Greek fathers had taught centuries earlier.[14]

The text of Genesis states that the man and his wife were created *in* the image of God. The image of God itself is identified for us in the NT. Paul points out that it is Christ who *is* the image of God (2 Cor. 4:4; Col. 1:15). In discussing the resurrection of the body, he compares Adam with the risen Christ. From Adam we inherit the image of the earthly, in weakness and mortality, whereas in the risen Christ we receive the image of the heavenly, under the direction and domination of the Holy Spirit (1 Cor. 15:45–49).[15] In Paul's thought, Christ as the second Adam *is* the image of God. Adam was created *in* Christ and then fell from that condition, but now, in grace, we are being renewed in the image of God, *in Christ the second Adam*, and thus in knowledge, righteousness, and holiness. This teaching is also presented by the author of Hebrews. In the first paragraph, the letter states that the Son by whom God has spoken his final and ultimate word is "the brightness of his [God's] glory and the express image of his being" (Heb. 1:3).

Therefore, from the very first, God's ultimate purpose was foundational to all that he did—all things were heading, under his direction, to the goal he had set for them, to be headed up under the lordship of Christ. The incarnation was planned from eternity as an integral part of the whole work of salvation in Christ. This is quite different from the speculative claim that Christ would have become incarnate even if Adam had not sinned; if the incarnation and atonement were determined eternally, as the Bible testifies, so, too, was the fall of Adam.

13. See 1 Cor. 11:7; James 3:9.
14. Philip Edgcumbe Hughes, *The True Image: The Origin and Destiny of Man in Christ* (Grand Rapids: Eerdmans, 1989), 281–86.
15. Richard B. Gaffin Jr., *The Centrality of the Resurrection: A Study in Paul's Soteriology* (Grand Rapids: Baker, 1978).

God and Man: Distinct yet Compatible

Because man was created in the image of God, he was made for communion with God, to rule God's creation on his behalf. This is clear from Genesis 1, where the man and his wife were given dominion over the earth, over all that God had created. Psalm 8:3–8 reflects on this truth poetically:

> When I look at your heavens, the work of your fingers,
> the moon and the stars, which you have set in place,
> what is man that you are mindful of him,
> and the son of man that you care for him?

> Yet you have made him a little lower than the heavenly beings
> and crowned him with glory and honor.
> You have given him dominion over the works of your hands;
> you have put all things under his feet,
> all sheep and oxen,
> and also the beasts of the field,
> the birds of the heavens, and the fish of the sea,
> whatever passes along the paths of the seas.

Man is therefore a creature, made by God, not eternal or intrinsically immortal but the highest creature, to whom and for whom the world was made. As a finite creature, he has been given the great privilege of governing the earth on behalf of his Creator. At the same time, he was also connected to God, made in his image and living in communion with him. The implication of Genesis 2 is that there was regular communication between God and Adam before the fall. God gave the man and the woman verbal charge to multiply and have dominion (Gen. 1:28–30), instructed Adam to abstain from the tree of the knowledge of good and evil, while being free to eat of all other trees in the garden (2:16), and brought to him the woman he had made for him (2:21–22). In rather different circumstances, after the fall, he addressed the errant pair (3:8ff.).

Therefore, on the one hand there is a *difference* between God and man. God is the Creator, man his creature. God is infinite and eternal, sovereign and all-powerful; man is weak and finite, a creature of time and space, limited to one place at one time, subject to the rule of God his Creator, derivative, not creative in the sense outlined in Genesis. The prophet Isaiah stresses this

point on many occasions, drawing attention to the uniqueness and supremacy
of Yahweh the God of Judah:

> Thus says the LORD, the King of Israel
>   and his Redeemer, the LORD of hosts:
> "I am the first and I am the last;
>   besides me there is no god.
> Who is like me? Let him proclaim it.
>   Let him declare and set it before me,
> since I appointed an ancient people.
>   Let them declare what is to come, and what will happen.
> Fear not, nor be afraid;
>   have I not told you from of old and declared it?
>   And you are my witnesses!
> Is there a God besides me?
>   There is no Rock; I know not any." (Isa. 44:6–8)

On the other hand, however, there is an inherent *compatibility* between
God and man. Man has been created *in* the image of God. He was made
for communion with his Creator. He was given responsibility for the earth,
accountable directly to God. He was placed in a situation in which word-
revelation was the normal manner of communication between himself and
the woman, and between himself and God. He was constituted by God a
covenant partner, given the freedom of the beautiful garden, granted clear-cut
responsibilities in it for the glory of God, warned about the consequences of
deviating from this task and misusing the creation in defiance of his God,
and so honored with moral qualities and responsibility. He was made for
God, and God condescended to him to be his partner in the task of world-
rule. Moreover, since all this was done with the express intention of the
incarnation of the Son (we will consider this topic in the next chapter), this
compatibility is demonstrably at the heart of God's intention for his creation
and for man himself.

The Fall: Unity Disrupted

Sin entered; Genesis 3 tells the sorry tale. Adam and his wife disobeyed
God's law and reaped the consequences, which are ultimately found in death.
One of the immediate results of human sin was a disrupted relationship with

the created order. Adam had been placed in the garden to till the ground, to bring it into subjection.[16] Now that sin had entered, Adam's work, intended as a blessing, became a curse. The land was to yield thorns and thistles. Work was to become hard labor. The fruits of human toil would be paltry in comparison with what they would and could have been (Gen. 3:14–19).

Hebrews 2:5–9 reflects on the poetic account of man's place in creation found in Psalm 8. God put everything under his feet. But we do not yet see everything subject to man. He has not yet achieved this goal. It is all too evident in the world around us. The environment is in a precarious position. Unwise governmental policies, unchecked exploitation of natural resources, disruptive and destructive wars, the repression of human enterprise by totalitarian dictatorships and meddlesome bureaucracies—these have all contributed to severe problems that affect the food chain, the quality of life, and much more. The major problem is that man cannot control himself. Constant strife, unchecked self-interest, societal breakdown, and violent religious fanaticism run rampant. Since man cannot even exercise discipline over his own inclinations, how can he bring the cosmos into godly subjection?

Yet we see Jesus, who for a little while was made lower than the angels in his incarnation and in the time of his lowliness from conception to the cross. He is now seated at the right hand of God, in authority over all things, fulfilling God's purpose for the human race at creation. The focus shifts in citing Psalm 8 from man in general to Jesus in particular.

> Now in putting everything in subjection to him, he left nothing outside his control. At present, we do not yet see everything in subjection to him. But we see Jesus who for a little while was made lower than the angels so that by the grace of God he might taste death for everyone, because of the suffering of death crowned with glory and honor. (Heb. 2:8b–9)[17]

He is the pioneer and perfecter of our faith who is bringing us there to share with him in the rule over the renovated cosmos. This we will do in union with him. Where the first Adam failed, having succumbed to the tempter and

16. This was an agricultural task, although there is good evidence that it was not limited to that but was primarily a function of a priest-king. See J. V. Fesko, *Last Things First* (Fearn, Ross-shire, UK: Mentor, 2007).

17. I have slightly amended the ESV translation and rendered the clauses in verse 9 in terms of the progression of thought of the author. The sentence is a chiasmus, with the first and last clauses connected and the inward clauses connected.

plunged himself and the race into sin, the second Adam prevailed, resisting the devil and by his obedience bringing those in union with him to the goal mapped out for them. John Henry Newman captures the idea in his hymn "Praise to the Holiest in the Height":

> O loving wisdom of our God, when all was sin and shame,
> A second Adam to the fight and to the rescue came.
>
> O wisest love, that flesh and blood which did in Adam fail,
> Should strive afresh against the foe, should strive and should prevail.

Union with Christ rests on the foundation of man's nature as created, seen in the light of God's end purpose for man. Christ as the second or last Adam achieves what the first Adam so signally failed to do. In view of this, the incarnation of Christ is crucial. It is the Archimedean point in this grand panorama. It is the theme of the next chapter.

Incarnation

Christ's Union with Humanity

The witness of the NT is that Jesus Christ is the eternal Son of God. Producing evidence in support of this claim is superfluous; it has been abundantly demonstrated to be the overwhelming theme throughout the Gospels and Epistles. John frames his Gospel with two great affirmations. In the prologue, he declares that the Logos who was in the beginning with God and was God, who created all things, became flesh and lived among us (John 1:1–4, 14–18). At the end, the climax of the document is Thomas's affirmation "My Lord and my God!" (20:28). In between, Jesus claims equality with God and defends himself against the charge of blasphemy on the grounds that he is telling the truth (5:16–47). Later, he goes one stage further by claiming identity with the Father, with the same consequences as before (10:22–36). He points to himself as coordinate with God as the object of faith (14:1), since he who has seen him has seen the Father (14:7–11). Indeed, he and the Father mutually indwell each other in the being of God (14:7–20; 17:21–24). In the Gospel of Matthew, he presents himself as having coordinate knowledge and sovereignty with God the Father (Matt. 11:25–27). Paul characteristically calls the risen Christ kurios ("Lord"), the Greek equivalent of the Hebrew adonai, used instead of YHWH for the God of Israel.[1]

Yet Jesus was also born, grew, and developed from infancy to childhood to adulthood. He was conceived by the Holy Spirit, and born of the

---

1. For a fuller exposition of Jesus as God, see Robert Letham, *The Holy Trinity: In Scripture, History, Theology, and Worship* (Phillipsburg, NJ: P&R Publishing, 2004), 34–51.

virgin Mary. The birth narratives in Matthew 1:18–25 and Luke 1:26–38 describe this in turn from the perspectives of Joseph and Mary. Both Gospels portray the Holy Spirit as responsible for Jesus' conception (Matt. 1:18; Luke 1:34–35), much to the astonishment of both Mary and her husband. There is evidence that other NT writers were aware of these events. Mark refers to Jesus as "the son of Mary" (Mark 6:3), in radical departure from the custom of naming a man as the son of his father. Paul, in Galatians 4:4, employs *ginesthai* ("to become") when writing of Jesus' birth, despite his otherwise invariable practice of using *gennan* for human begetting, three occurrences of which are present in this same chapter. Both Mark and Paul suggest that they are aware of something very unusual about Jesus' birth. Again, while the united evidence of NT manuscripts supports a plural reading in John 1:13, with John referring to the regeneration of believers, Tertullian—at the beginning of the third century—claims that this resulted from the Valentinians' tampering with the text, which should instead be read as singular and as a reference not to believers but to Jesus, who was born "not of blood, nor of the will of the flesh, nor of the will of man, but of God." Whatever one's conclusions about the original reading, the point is established that at this very early stage it was strongly recognized that Jesus was born of the virgin.[2]

Jesus' humanity is real and genuine. The Gospels present him as growing to adulthood in a normal way (Luke 2:40–52). He experienced weariness and thirst, hunger and sleep (John 4:4–7; 19:28; Matt. 4:1–2; 8:24). He had a circle of friends: Peter, James, and John within the apostolic circle, Mary, Martha, and Lazarus at Bethany. He was apparently a convivial companion, creating vintage wine for a wedding banquet when supplies ran out and enjoying food and alcoholic beverages like everyone else in first-century Israel (John 2:1–11; Matt. 11:19); this is hardly surprising, since when young he had grown in favor with his contemporaries (Luke 2:52). He took his family responsibilities seriously, entrusting his mother to the care of the apostle John when he was on the point of death (John 19:25–27). He knew sorrow, disturbed by death and weeping with grief at the grave of Lazarus (John 11:32–38). Earlier, his legal father, Joseph, had died. The author of Hebrews stresses that Jesus shared with us flesh and blood, faith, temptation, sufferings, and death (Heb. 2:5–18), prayed to the Father in deep anguish, and was tested in all points

---

2. I am indebted for these observations to Thomas F. Torrance, *Incarnation: The Person and Life of Christ* (Milton Keynes, UK: Paternoster, 2008), 88–94.

as we are (Heb. 4:14–5:10). He was buried in a tomb (Matt. 27:57–66; Mark 15:43–47; Luke 23:50–56; John 19:38–42).

All this was "for us and our salvation," as the Niceno-Constantinopolitan creed puts it. God alone is the Savior, and it is futile to rely on man (Ps. 146:1ff.). Yet God alone could not save us! This startling reality is affirmed by Heidelberg Catechism 16; since God is just, man's sin required atonement by man: "the same human nature which has sinned should make satisfaction for sin." Thus, in the words of John Henry Newman in his hymn "Praise to the Holiest in the Height":

> O loving wisdom of our God, when all was sin and shame,
> A second Adam to the fight and to the rescue came.
>
> O wisest love, that flesh and blood which did in Adam fail,
> Should strive afresh against the foe, should strive and should prevail.
>
> And that a higher gift than grace should flesh and blood refine,
> God's presence and his very self, and essence all divine.

The Eternal Son of God Unites to Himself a Human Nature

The basis of our union with Christ is Christ's union with us in the incarnation. We can become one with him because he first became one with us. By taking human nature into personal union, the Son of God has joined himself to humanity. He now has a human body and soul, which he will never jettison.

In the prologue to his Gospel, John declares that the same Word who is eternal, who was in the beginning, who was with God, and who is God became flesh and lived among us (John 1:1–4, 14–18). This becoming flesh was not a transformation into something other than who he eternally is. He remained unchanging. He was still the Word, and remained so even as the disciples saw his glory. He added humanity and lived and acted as man, yet he remained God. The Word himself takes the initiative, comes into this world and takes flesh into union.

This is Paul's stress also in 2 Corinthians 5:19, when he writes that "God was in Christ reconciling the world to himself"; God is the active agent. God was in Christ. God in Christ is the personal agent who recon-ciles the world. Therefore, the human aspect was and is the humanity of the Son of God. In Galatians 4:4, Paul records that God the Father sent his Son at the appointed time. His humanity is real. He underwent a real conception, gestation, and birth—"born of woman." Paul seems to recognize a certain unusualness about the conception, for again, instead of his normal verb for "generation," *gennan*, he uses *ginesthai*. Nevertheless, Jesus' birth was entirely normal, with nothing out of the ordinary. He "became of a woman." Moreover, he was placed under the law, as a Jew in the context of the covenant relationship established by Yahweh with Israel. The context of chapter 3 describes the covenantal state of Israel as at that time in its minority. Jesus was born into that situation, and his life was circumscribed by the Mosaic law and all it required.

Other passages in Paul's letters say the same thing from differing angles. In Romans 8:3, Paul declares that because of the law's inability to change people's lives, exacerbated by their sinful nature, which led to its continual breach, "God sent forth his Son in the likeness of sinful flesh and for sin." Paul certainly does not intend to say that Christ was merely like us, his humanity less than full and real. The "likeness" (*homoiōma*) indicates his appearance, viewed in comparison to the "flesh of sin" of his contemporaries. He was human, like his fellow human beings, who themselves were sinners. In his case, he came in order to condemn "sin in the flesh." Again, it is the Son of the Father who identifies himself with other humans to the fullest extent, sin apart. In Philippians 2:6ff., Paul adds to this that Christ, being (*huparchōn*: present participle, denoting continuance throughout) in the form of God, added the form of a servant, becoming obedient to the death of the cross. He continued in the form of God, equal to God, but added the lowliness of a servant, being found in the appearance of a man.

The Letter to the Hebrews reinforces this consistent theme. After devoting the first chapter to establishing the eternal deity of the Son, his supremacy over the prophets and the angels, the author underlines his genuine humanity in chapter 2. He shares with us flesh and blood, faith, the experience of temptation, suffering, and ultimately death. As with Paul, the subject of these circumstances is the same as the One who created all things and upholds the universe; it is the Son through whom God has spoken his final culminating word of salvation (Heb. 2:5–18; cf. 1:1–14), who prayed to the Father with loud cries and tears (4:14–5:10).

Excursus: The Development of Christological Thought to the Second Council of Constantinople (A.D. 553)[3]

The Nestorian Crisis and the Council of Ephesus (431)

In the early fifth century, a major crisis arose over the identity of Jesus Christ. Since he was and is the eternal Son of God, how does this relate to the fact—obvious from the Gospels—that he is also human? Flowing from this, what significance do these things have for our salvation? These questions were thrust into the foreground in the year 428 by Nestorius, the bishop of Constantinople.[4] He began to attack the term *theotokos* ("God-bearer"), a popular title for Mary. Since he distinguished sharply between the deity of Christ and his humanity,[5] he held that Mary could strictly be called only mother of *the man* Jesus. She could be termed *christotokos* ("Christ-bearer") with no qualms, since in this there was no danger of confusing deity and humanity. Talk of Mary as *theotokos* conjured up in his mind the specter of Arianism. Arios, and his more influential successor Eunomios, had reduced the Son's deity to creaturehood. Nestorius feared that use of *theotokos* would lead to a blurring of the Creator-creature distinction. He wanted to avoid any notion of a mixture of deity and humanity, and so his aim was to preserve the integrity of the human nature. He was also alert to the danger of Apollinarianism. Apollinaris (c. 315–before 392), a strong supporter of the Council of Nicaea, had wandered into heresy in his old age by teaching that the Logos took the place of a human soul in the incarnate Christ. The Word assumed flesh—a body—only. He was condemned by the first Council of Constantinople (381). The problem with Apollinaris's teaching, in Gregory Nazianzen's words, was that "whatever is not assumed cannot be healed."[6] If the Son did not assume into union a full humanity, including a soul, there was no incarnation. We could not then be saved, because Christ would have been less than man, since a human being minus a soul is not a human being. Nestorius's concern was—correctly—to affirm the full integrity of Christ's

---

3. Much of the substance of this section first appeared in my book *Through Western Eyes: Eastern Orthodoxy; A Reformed Perspective* (Fearn, Ross-shire, UK: Mentor, 2007) and is printed here with permission. See http://www.christianfocus.com.

4. On Nestorius, see G. L. Prestige, *Fathers and Heretics* (London: SPCK, 1940), 120–49; J. N. D. Kelly, *Early Christian Doctrines* (London: Adam & Charles Black, 1968), 310–17.

5. See D. S. Wallace-Hadrill, *Christian Antioch: A Study of Early Christian Thought in the East* (Cambridge: Cambridge University Press, 1982).

6. Gregory of Nazianzus, *Epistola 101, PG* 31:181c.

human nature. His problem was that while he had a firm grasp of the distinctiveness of Christ's divinity and humanity, he was less sure of the unity of his person. So he spoke of a "conjunction" of the divinity and humanity rather than a "union," a conjunction that resulted in a *prosōpon* of union, a single object of appearance, which was identical with neither of the two natures. The *prosōpon* of union, not the Logos or Word, was the subject of the incarnate Christ.

Nestorius was vehemently opposed by Cyril of Alexandria, who began from the premise of Christ's unity.[7] For Cyril, Nestorius threatened not only the unity of Christ's person but also the incarnation itself, for his teaching effectively denied that there was a real participation by the Son of God in our humanity. The two natures—so it seemed—were more like two pieces of board held together by glue. Cyril stressed that salvation was a work of God, that the man Jesus could not defeat sin and death by his human nature alone. To do this, the eternal Logos assumed into *union* the human nature of Christ.[8]

In his *Second Letter to Nestorius*, Cyril starts with the unity of Christ's person. The Word "united to himself . . . flesh enlivened by a rational soul, and in this way became a human being." There is an "unspeakable and unutterable convergence into unity, one Christ and one Son out of two." To reject this personal union is to fall into the error of positing two sons. "We do not worship a human being in conjunction with the Logos, lest the appearance of a division creep in . . . No, we worship one and the same, because the body of the Logos is not alien to him but accompanies him even as he is enthroned with the Father." The Word did not unite himself to a human person but to flesh. The virgin Mary is *theotokos*, since it is *the Word* that united himself to this human body and soul.[9] In short, Cyril Nestorius's stress on the integrity and distinctiveness of Christ's humanity had jeopardized his unity.

In his *Third Letter to Nestorius*, Cyril again stresses the personal union of the Word with the flesh. All expressions in the Gospels refer to *the one*

---

7. For Cyril, see St. Cyril of Alexandria, *On the Unity of Christ*, ed. John Anthony McGuckin (Crestwood, NY: St. Vladimir's Seminary Press, 1995); John Anthony McGuckin, *St. Cyril of Alexandria and the Christological Controversy: Its History, Theology, and Texts* (Crestwood, NY: St. Vladimir's Seminary Press, 2004); Prestige, *Fathers*, 150–79; Kelly, *Doctrines*, 317–23; Norman Russell, *Cyril of Alexandria* (London: Routledge, 2000).

8. See John Meyendorff, *Christ in Eastern Christian Thought* (Crestwood, NY: St. Vladimir's Seminary Press, 1975), 18–19.

9. Leo Donald Davis, *The First Seven Ecumenical Councils (325–787)* (Collegeville, MN: Liturgical Press, 1990), 149–50; Richard A. Norris Jr., *The Christological Controversy* (Philadelphia: Fortress Press, 1980), 131–35, esp. 133.

incarnate person of the Word. Mary is *theotokos* because she "gave birth after the flesh to God who was united by *hypostasis* with flesh," man ensouled with a rational soul.[10] Cyril adds twelve anathemas to this letter. In these, he declares that "if anyone will not confess that the Emmanuel is very God, and that therefore the Holy Virgin is the Mother of God [*theotokos*], inasmuch as in the flesh she bore the Word of God made flesh . . . ; let him be anathema." He insists, inter alia, that it is the Word who suffered, was crucified, and died according to the flesh.[11] For Cyril, the Word who existed before the incarnation is the same person after the incarnation, now enfleshed. This union excludes division but does not eliminate difference.

The council called to Ephesus to resolve the matter expelled Nestorius from the episcopal office and the priesthood.[12] The council declared that Christ's humanity, wholly human, was appropriated by the Word as his own, and so forms the basis for our own salvation.[13]

Eutyches and the Council of Chalcedon[14]

Before long a fresh crisis arose, generated by Eutyches from Alexandria, whom Kelly calls an "aged and muddle-headed archimandrite."[15] Eutyches is an extreme exponent of Cyrilline Christology, without Cyril's theological sophistication. For Eutyches, before the incarnation Christ was of two natures but after it he is one nature, one Christ, one Son, in one *hypostasis* and one *prosōpon*. Christ's flesh was not identical with ordinary human flesh, since Eutyches thought this would entail the Word's assuming an individual man, thus destroying the union. Behind this, he understood nature to mean concrete existence—so Christ could not have two natures or he would have two concrete existences and so be divided.[16] Thus, Eutyches had an overpowering emphasis on the unity of Christ's person, exactly the opposite of

10. Edward Rochie Hardy, *Christology of the Later Fathers*, Library of Christian Classics (Philadelphia: Westminster Press, 1954), 349–54, esp. 352–53.

11. Ibid., 354; Davis, *Councils*, 150–51; Henry R. Percival, *The Seven Ecumenical Councils of the Undivided Church: Their Canons and Dogmatic Decrees*, Select Library of Nicene and Post-Nicene Fathers of the Christian Church, 2nd ser. (Edinburgh: T&T Clark, 1997), 206.

12. Davis, *Councils*, 160.

13. Meyendorff, *Christ*, 21.

14. See Aloys Grillmeier, S.J., *Christ in Christian Tradition*, vol. 1, *From the Apostolic Age to Chalcedon (451)*, trans. John Bowden, 2nd rev. ed. (Atlanta: John Knox Press, 1975), 520–57; Jaroslav Pelikan, *The Christian Tradition*, vol. 1, *The Emergence of the Catholic Tradition (100–600)* (Chicago: University of Chicago Press, 1971), 263–66.

15. Kelly, *Doctrines*, 331.

16. See ibid., 330–34; Davis, *Councils*, 171.

Nestorius. Whereas Nestorius had sought to uphold the distinctness of the two natures and so threatened the unity of Christ, Eutyches so underlined Christ's unity that he blurred the distinctness of the two natures, his humanity swamped by his deity, although to be fair he did insist on the full and complete humanity. His ideas raised problems similar to those of Apollinaris, for our salvation depends on the reality of the incarnation, of a real assumption of unabbreviated humanity by the Son of God. If Christ were not truly and fully man, we could not be saved, for only a second Adam could undo the damage caused by the first.

Eventually Marcian, the emperor, called a council to be held at Nicaea in 451, to which Pope Leo sent three legates.[17] But because of invasions by the Huns, the emperor ordered the council to move to Chalcedon, across the Bosphorus. The bishops reaffirmed Cyril's *Second Letter to Nestorius* and Leo's *Tome*.[18] A commission was appointed to draw up a doctrinal statement. In composing the Definition, the bishops drew on a variety of sources, Leo's *Tome* the single most decisive contributor, even though there were more quotations from Cyril.[19] The Definition clearly distinguishes between one person and two natures:

> Therefore, following the holy Fathers, we all with one accord teach men to acknowledge one and the same Son, our Lord Jesus Christ, at once complete in Godhead and complete in manhood, truly God and truly man, consisting also of a reasonable soul and body; of one substance with the Father as regards his Godhead, and at the same time of one substance with us as regards his manhood; like us in all respects, apart from sin; as regards his Godhead, begotten of the Father before the ages, but yet as regards his manhood begotten, for us and for our salvation, of Mary the Virgin, the God-bearer; one and the same Christ, Son, Lord, Only-begotten, recognized in two natures, without confusion, without change, without division, without separation; the distinction of natures being in no way annulled by the union, but rather the characteristics of each nature being preserved and coming together to form one person and subsistence, not as parted or

17. For the Council of Chalcedon, see R. V. Sellers, *The Council of Chalcedon: A Historical and Doctrinal Survey* (London: SPCK, 1953), 209ff.; Kelly, *Doctrines*, 338–43; Davis, *Councils*, 180–82; Percival, *Seven Ecumenical Councils*, 243–95.

18. After Leo's *Tome* was read, at the second session of the council, "the most reverend bishops cried out: This is the faith of the fathers, this is the faith of the apostles. So we all believe, thus the orthodox believe. Anathema to him who does not thus believe. Peter has spoken thus through Leo. So taught the apostles." Percival, *Seven Ecumenical Councils*, 259.

19. Pelikan, *Catholic Tradition*, 263–64; Sellers, *Chalcedon*, 209–10.

separated into two persons, but one and the same Son and only-begotten God, the Word, Lord Jesus Christ; even as the prophets from earliest times spoke of him, and our Lord Jesus Christ himself taught us, and the creed of the Fathers has handed down to us.[20]

That Christ subsists in two natures is a decisive rejection of Eutyches. The Definition rejects any notion of the union that might erode or threaten the differences of the natures. At the same time, it also insists that Christ is not divided or separated into two persons, as the Nestorian heresy implied.

The anti-Nestorian stance is evident in a number of ways. The repetition of the phrase "the same" and the reaffirmation of the virgin Mary as *theotokos* are two obvious points. Again, toward the end, the Definition denies that Christ is parted or separated into two persons, but rather asserts that the two natures "come together to form one person and subsistence," echoing Cyril's *Second Letter to Nestorius*. In all these it clearly affirms the unity of the person of Christ. On the other hand, the Definition equally repudiates the Eutychian heresy, which had occasioned the council in the first place. Christ is "complete in manhood," so much so that he is "of one substance with us." The distinction of natures is in no way annulled by the union. There are also clear restatements of opposition both to Apollinarianism, in the point that Christ has "a reasonable soul and body," and also to Arianism, in that Christ is "of one substance with the Father."

Above all, the famous four privative adverbs together form the central hinge of the Definition. The incarnate Christ is "*in two natures, without confusion, without change.*" Here is an explicit rejection of Eutyches. The union neither changes Christ's humanity into anything else nor absorbs it into the divinity. The humanity remains fully humanity. On the other side of the spectrum, the natures are "*without division, without separation.*" By this it is declared impermissible so to focus on either nature of Christ that the personal union is undermined in the manner Nestorius had done. These four adverbs outlaw both Nestorianism and Eutychianism.

The council also anathematizes those who talk of two natures of the Lord before the union but only one afterward. This is directed at Eutyches, probably at the behest of Pope Leo and the papal legates.[21] It was to cause problems later

---

20. See Henry Bettenson, ed., *Documents of the Christian Church*, 2nd ed. (London: Oxford University Press, 1963), 51–52.
21. Sellers, *Chalcedon*, 224–26.

for the Monophysites (those who held to "one nature"), who were accustomed to think of *nature* as synonymous with what we would now call *person* and for whom Chalcedon seemed an unwarranted capitulation to Nestorius. The problem, however, was more a lack of knowledge of Greek by the Latins, who had pressed this point. Taking *phusis* (Greek) to mean *natura* (Latin), it seemed to Leo and his legates that the Alexandrian mantra of one incarnate nature (*phusis*) of the Logos was a heretical belief in only one *natura*. It betrayed a failure to appreciate that at this time the Greeks were using *phusis* and *hypostasis* interchangeably. It was to be another century before Emperor Justinian I brought about a clear distinction between these two terms. In reality, the true objection in this anathema is, as Sellers observes, to Eutyches's false interpretation of the formula, not to Cyril's position, which was not in view at the time.[22]

Assessment of Chalcedon

Chalcedon failed to do justice to some real concerns of the Cyrillians. The point that "the distinction of natures being in no way annulled by the union but rather the characteristics of each nature being preserved and coming together" could be taken to mean that human attributes must be predicated only of the human nature, and the divine of the divine. This sounded Nestorian to these people. It gave the impression that Christ was some form of schizoid, for whom some things could be related only to one part of him and other things to another part. Their strong concern for the unity of Christ seemed to have been given short shrift. It seemed as though the idea that salvation begun by the union of the human nature of Christ with the divine was under attack. Chalcedon certainly allows the deity and humanity to be seen as two, each in its "ownness."[23]

Moreover, Chalcedon left the concept of the hypostatic union unclear. For instance, it did not specify *who* exactly it was who had suffered and been crucified. Nor did it say—a vital theme for Cyril's supporters—that the deification of man began in the union of Christ's humanity with his divinity. The Monophysites later thought that Chalcedon was soft on Nestorianism by asserting "two natures after the union," precisely because it made no mention of the hypostatic union, refusing to include the confession "out of two." Chalcedon satisfied the West but not the East.[24]

22. Ibid., 226.
23. Ibid., 224.
24. Ibid., 256–60; Davis, *Councils*, 187; Meyendorff, *Christ*, 28; Pelikan, *Catholic Tradition*, 265–66.

Furthermore, two passages in Leo's *Tome*, effectively canonized by Chalcedon, were held by the Monophysites to be indisputably Nestorian, where "Leo so separates, and personalizes, what is divine and what is human in Christ that the hypostatic union is dissolved."[25] Leo states that the properties of both natures are kept intact so that "one and the same mediator between God and human beings, the human being who is Jesus Christ, can at one and the same time die in virtue of the one nature and, in virtue of the other, be incapable of death."[26] In the absence of mention of the hypostatic union, followers of Cyril were loath to accept Chalcedon. Moreover, they strongly held to the personal identity of the incarnate Christ with the preexistent Son, and this the council did not affirm,[27] although the repeated phrase "one and the same" must be borne in mind in response to this claim.

Chalcedon was never intended to be the final definitive verdict on Christology. As Sellers points out, "it allows deductions to be made from its dogmatic decisions, and, in effect, encourages enquiry into the mystery."[28] "It is intended to explain just one definite question of the church's christology, indeed the most important one. It does not lay claim to having said all that may be said about Christ." It was far from innovative, but rather was in line with the preceding tradition. "Few councils have been so rooted in tradition as the Council of Chalcedon. The dogma of Chalcedon is ancient tradition in a formula corresponding to the needs of the hour. So we cannot say that the Chalcedonian Definition marks a great turning point in the christological belief of the early church."[29] At the same time, it left a good deal of unfinished business on the table.

The Monophysites and Constantinople II (553)[30]

As a consequence of Ephesus and Chalcedon, sections of the church went into a schism that still continues. This breakup occurred over whether

25. Sellers, *Chalcedon*, 266.

26. Norris, *Controversy*, 148.

27. Davis, *Councils*, 196–97.

28. Sellers, *Chalcedon*, 350.

29. Grillmeier, *From the Apostolic Age to Chalcedon*, 550.

30. Ibid., 438–75, 503–13; Sellers, *Chalcedon*, 254–350; Herbert M. Relton, *A Study in Christology: The Problem of the Relation of the Two Natures in the Person of Christ* (London: SPCK, 1917); Timothy Ware, *The Orthodox Church* (London: Penguin Books, 1969), 37; Jaroslav Pelikan, *The Christian Tradition*, vol. 2, *The Spirit of Eastern Christendom* (Chicago: University of Chicago Press, 1974), 49–61; Pelikan, *Catholic Tradition*, 277, 337–41; W. H. C. Frend, *The Rise of the Monophysite Movement* (Cambridge: Cambridge University Press, 1972); Meyendorff, *Christ*.

the Chalcedonian formula, by its stress on the integrity of the two natures and the appropriate attributions to be made to either one, actually left the door open to a Nestorian interpretation that undermined the unity of Christ's person. Many thought this was exactly what it did do. They were disconcerted that not nearly enough emphasis was laid on Christ's unity and on his personal identity with the eternal, preexistent Logos. These people, the Monophysites, took as their lodestar Cyril's phrase "the one incarnate nature of the Word made flesh."

The foundational point of disagreement between the Monophysites and the Chalcedonians surrounded the unity of Christ and the place accorded to his human nature. The Monophysites insisted on the absolute unity of the person of Christ and his continuity with the preincarnate Logos. The Chalcedonians, on the other hand, were fearful of minimizing the humanity of Christ and could never accept that Christ's manhood was merely a "state" of the Logos.

Leontius of Byzantium[31]

Leontius shared the Alexandrian stress on Christ's unity, but he was also concerned to preserve the true humanity.[32] He came up with the idea of Christ's humanity as *enhypostatos* (existing in a *hypostasis*—roughly, "person"—of another nature). Christ's human nature subsists in the *hypostasis* of the divine nature. Thus, the human nature in Christ is both *anhypostatos*—having no existence of its own independently[33]—and also *enhypostatos*—subsisting *in* a *hypostasis* of another nature. The single *hypostasis* ("person") of Christ is the eternal Word in which are two natures, divine and human. All operations of both natures are attributed to the *hypostasis* ("person") of the divine Word.[34] Grillmeier considers this the work of Leontius of Jerusalem, further developed by Emperor Justinian. Both Relton and Sellers take the older view that Leontius of Byzantium propounded *enhypostasia*.[35] For

---

31. Aloys Grillmeier, S.J., *Christ in Christian Tradition*, vol. 2, *From the Council of Chalcedon (451) to Gregory the Great (590–604)*, pt. 2, *The Church of Constantinople in the Sixth Century*, trans. John Cawte (London: Mowbray, 1995), 181–229; Relton, *A Study in Christology*, 69–83; Brian Daley, "Leontius of Byzantium: A Critical Edition of His Works, with Prolegomena" (D.Phil. diss., Oxford University, 1978).

32. Davis, *Councils*, 221.

33. This is often rather unhelpfully called "the impersonal humanity." Of course, it is impossible to contemplate humanity that does not have personhood. What this idea attests is that the assumed humanity of Christ exists only as the humanity of the Son of God. In turn, *enhypostasia* underlines the point that this humanity *is* that of the eternal Son of the Father.

34. Davis, *Councils*, 234; Meyendorff, *Christ*, 61–68.

35. Sellers, *Chalcedon*, 308–20, esp. 316–19; Relton, *A Study in Christology*, 69–83.

Leontius of Byzantium, we have translated extracts from *Three Books against the Nestorians and Eutychians* (his chief work).[36]

Leontius of Jerusalem[37]

The other Leontius, whose contribution to the debate occurred between 532 and 536, was emphatic that the one subject in Christ is clearly the *hypostasis* ("person") of the Logos. This was, of course, something to which Chalcedon could not have aspired.[38] Grillmeier comments that "there is thus complete identity of the *prosōpon*, of the person, of the subject before and after the incarnation. The pre-existent *hypostasis* of the Logos himself is the subject of the incarnation who assumes a human nature, which neither is nor has its own *prosōpon* . . . Because the one *hypostasis* has entered into this entitative relationship with the *prosōpon*-less *sarx*, it can bear both series of 'physical names,' that is, the predicates of both divine and human natures."[39] He continues, "Thus it follows that the acknowledgement of divinity and humanity in Christ as *enhypostata* does not mean that they are *idiohypostata*, that is, that each constitutes its own proper *hypostasis*. For Leontius of Jerusalem, Christ is only one *hypostasis* in the real two natures."[40] Indeed, he wrote that the Word hypostatized human nature into his own hypostasis.[41]

Leontius of Jerusalem makes a real contribution insofar as the concept of *enhypostasis* or insubsistence emerges formally and is used to explain the unity of the subject in Christ.[42] Moreover, Meyendorff sums up by explaining Leontius's meaning as "a hypostasis that, instead of being another isolated and individualized hypostasis among all the hypostases that constitute the human nature, is the hypostatic archetype of the whole of mankind, in whom 'recapitulated' mankind, and not merely an individual, recovers union with God. This is possible only if Christ's manhood is not the human nature of a mere man but that of a hypostasis independent of the limitations of created nature."[43] In this, Leontius was providing the foundations for a coherent doctrine of union with Christ and deification. The assumed humanity,

---

36. Hardy, *Later Fathers*, 375–77.
37. Grillmeier, *The Church of Constantinople in the Sixth Century*, 276–312.
38. Ibid., 277.
39. Ibid., 279.
40. Ibid., 285.
41. Cited in Meyendorff, *Christ*, 74.
42. Grillmeier, *The Church of Constantinople in the Sixth Century*, 289.
43. Meyendorff, *Christ*, 75.

deified in and by the Word, becomes the source of divine life, since it is the Word's own flesh. Because Christ's humanity has divine life hypostatically, we can—in union with Christ—receive divine life by grace and participation.[44] This is a crucial point and one that we will face when we consider Calvin's contribution to union with Christ, particularly as it is focused in the Lord's Supper. Since Christ's human nature is the human nature of the eternal Son of God, it is suffused by the divine qualities of the Son, *while remaining human*.[45] The East claims that the flesh or humanity of Christ was deified by participation in the Son of God. The biblical evidence for this, among other places, is evident in the word of the angel in Luke 1:34–35 that the Holy Spirit, in overshadowing Mary and bringing about the new creation in the conception of Jesus, would also effect the result that he would be called "the holy Son of God."

Justinian I

The third contributor to the resolution of the post-Chalcedon Christological problem was the Emperor Justinian I (483–565, emperor from 527). In many ways, he is the principal architect of the conclusion of the crisis at Constantinople II. His interest in theology propelled him onto the stage as a force to be reckoned with theologically as well as politically. He was no mere dilettante. He was a man "orthodox and deeply pious with a taste for theological discussion." He intervened forcefully in ecclesiastical matters more than any emperor before. He recognized that the formula of the Scythian monks "one of the trinity suffered for us" (designed to smoke out any with Nestorian sympathies) was true to Chalcedon and at the same time likely to

44. Ibid., 78–79; Leontius of Jerusalem, *Against Nestorius*, PG 86:1512b. But see Andrew Louth, *John Damascene: Tradition and Originality in Byzantine Theology* (Oxford: Oxford University Press, 2002), 160–61.

45. This statement is based on my reading of the patristic source. Bill Evans has pointed out to me the penetrating observations of Bruce McCormack to the effect that for Reformed theology the Holy Spirit, not the hypostatic union, preserves the incarnate Christ from the taint of sin. This is indeed so, as I have myself affirmed elsewhere. Robert Letham, *The Work of Christ* (Leicester, UK: Inter-Varsity Press, 1993), 114–15; Letham, *The Holy Trinity*, 56–57. But the work of the Holy Spirit and the personalization of the Incarnate One by the eternal Son are not at loggerheads as if they were from disparate sources. The Son and the Spirit act distinctly, yet harmoniously and indivisibly, in all the ways and works of God. Both are involved—with this distinction: the assumed humanity is in *personal union* not with the Holy Spirit but with the eternal Son. See Bruce L. McCormack, *For Us and Our Salvation: Incarnation and Atonement in the Reformed Tradition*, Studies in Reformed Theology and History (Princeton: Princeton Theological Seminary, 1993), 17–22. Evans discusses this question himself in William B. Evans, *Imputation and Impartation: Union with Christ in American Reformed Theology* (Eugene, OR: Wipf & Stock, 2008), 167–68.

win over Cyril's supporters among the Monophysites. Moreover, the pope approved it, effectively providing the backing of the Western church.[46]

Between 532 and 536, Leontius of Jerusalem insisted on identifying the *hypostasis* of union in the incarnate Christ with the preexistent *hypostasis* of the Word. Christ's manhood had no preexistence, for "the *hypostasis* of Christ is the Divine Logos, One of the Holy Trinity."[47] Jesus *is* the second person of the Trinity, incarnate.[48] Thus *hypostasis* ("person"), not nature, is the foundation of being, entailing a *personal* foundation of reality and that God is primarily love.[49] It also means that the single *hypostasis* in Christ was the *hypostasis* of *both* the divine *and* human natures. Christ's humanity had no separate *hypostasis* of its own, so as a consequence Christ unites all mankind—not merely a single human being—to the divinity.

Justinian thereby established the distinction between *hypostasis* and nature. This clarified Chalcedon (the union of two natures in one *hypostasis*) by identifying the *hypostasis* of Christ as the preexistent *hypostasis* of the divine Word.[50] In short, the person of Jesus Christ *is* the eternal Son of God, now incarnate.

The Edict of Justinian: "The Edict on the True Faith" (551)

In this edict, Justinian explained his own view. It also presents the reasoning behind the fifth ecumenical council's decisions. The emperor set forth the orthodox doctrine, stating that "we confess that our Lord Jesus Christ is one and the same Divine Logos of God who was incarnate and became man."[51] In this he affirms the central point of the Cyrilline Christology and its development along the lines of the two Leontii. He enlarges on this by saying that "the *hypostatic* union means that the Divine Logos, that is to say one *hypostasis* of the three divine *hypostases*, is not united to a man who has his own *hypostasis* before [the union], but that in the womb of the Holy Virgin the Divine Logos made for himself, in his own *hypostasis*, flesh that was taken from her and that was endowed with a reasonable and intellectual soul, i.e., human nature."[52]

46. Davis, *Councils*, 225–29.
47. Kenneth Paul Wesche, *On the Person of Christ: The Christology of Emperor Justinian* (Crestwood, NY: St. Vladimir's Seminary Press, 1991), 12.
48. Ibid., 31, from Justinian's "Letter to the Monks of Alexandria against the Monophysites."
49. Ibid., 13–14.
50. Davis, *Councils*, 232.
51. Wesche, *The Christology of Justinian*, 165.
52. Ibid., 166.

Justinian argues that Cyril maintained the integrity of the two natures but that he used *nature* as a synonym for *hypostasis* ("person"). Instead, the emperor clearly distinguishes between the two terms. We cannot talk of Christ's having one nature and one hypostasis, but "we speak of one *hypostasis* and of a union of two natures," since the Logos of God was united to human nature and not to a particular *hypostasis*. So the one hypostasis of the Logos was incarnate and is recognized in both natures.[53] Thus, "we never refer to the human nature of Christ by itself, nor did it ever possess its own *hypostasis* or *prosōpon*, but it began to exist in the *hypostasis* of the Logos."[54] On the other hand, those who forbid talk of two natures after the union—such as Apollinaris and Eutyches—confuse the issue.[55]

Synthesis is the key to Justinian's Christology, union according to the *hypostasis*.[56] He says the divine *hypostasis* created this spiritually ensouled human nature for himself so as to be *hypostasis* for it and to exist humanly in it as divine *hypostasis*. In contrast to Chalcedon, which used *hypostasis* to refer to the outcome of the two natures coming together into one Christ, Justinian used it of the preexistent Logos. The assumed human nature thus participates in a *hypostasis* only by existing in the *hypostasis* of the Logos, by virtue of a creative act of the Logos himself.[57] Grillmeier remarks that Justinian had "a commendable understanding of the problems of incarnational theology" and that "in Justinian we find for the first time the sketch of a complete interpretation of Christ's person and its union of divine and human nature in the one divine *hypostasis* of the Logos."[58] While he bases his edict on Chalcedon, he has a stronger grasp of the union, resulting from the presence of Cyrilline elements and the model provided by Leontius of Jerusalem.

Justinian shared with the Monophysites the principle that Jesus Christ is the divine Logos. The main problem was that the Monophysites used *nature* as a synonym for *hypostasis* when talking of the particular but used *nature* as a synonym for *essence* (being) when talking of the universal. Justinian's achievement was to distinguish *nature* and *hypostasis* according to the Trinitarian distinction of the Cappadocians. *Hypostasis* refers

53. Ibid., 178.
54. Ibid., 179.
55. Ibid., 180.
56. Grillmeier, *The Church of Constantinople in the Sixth Century*, 435–36.
57. Ibid., 436–37.
58. Ibid., 438.

to the one Logos, who becomes man, and *nature* to the mystery that he became fully man.[59]

The Second Council of Constantinople (553)

Justinian called the council, explaining its purpose in a letter read at its first session as "to unite the churches again, and to bring the Synod of Chalcedon, together with the three earlier, to universal acceptance."[60] A series of anathemas stressed the unity of Christ, and another series defended the distinction (but not separation or division) of the natures.[61]

Canon II ascribes two births to the God-Logos, the one from eternity from the Father, without time and without body, and the other his being made flesh of the holy and glorious Mary, Mother of God. The next three canons are all strongly anti-Nestorian. Canon III says that the God-Logos who works miracles and the Christ who suffered should not be separated, for it is one and the same Jesus Christ our Lord, the Word, who became flesh and a human being.[62] Behind this is the fact that Christ's unity is a true union, not a mingling or division. Canon V asserts that there is only one subsistence or person. The incarnation is to be seen solely from the hypostasis of the Son, who is one of the Trinity. Thus "one of the trinity has been made man." Canon VIII, on the other hand, guards against Monophysitism, pronouncing that both natures remain what they were: "For in teaching that the only-begotten Word was united hypostatically [to humanity] we do not mean to say that there was made a mutual confusion of natures, but rather each [nature] remaining what it was, we understand that the Word was united to flesh."[63] Canon IX declares that the worshiping of Christ in two natures is in fact one act of worship directed to the incarnate God-Logos with his flesh.[64] Grillmeier concludes that Constantinople II is "not a weakening of Chalcedonian terminology, but its logical clarification . . . Nevertheless the use and application of the main concepts were clearer and more unambiguous than at Chalcedon."[65]

59. Wesche, *The Christology of Justinian*, 19–20.

60. Percival, *Seven Ecumenical Councils*, 302.

61. Davis, *Councils*, 244–46; Sellers, *Chalcedon*, 330; Hardy, *Later Fathers*, 378–81.

62. Grillmeier, *The Church of Constantinople in the Sixth Century*, 446; Percival, *Seven Ecumenical Councils*, 312.

63. Percival, *Seven Ecumenical Councils*, 313.

64. Ibid., 314–16; Grillmeier, *The Church of Constantinople in the Sixth Century*, 447–53.

65. Grillmeier, *The Church of Constantinople in the Sixth Century*, 456.

Summary of the Christological Crisis

In summary, the church's mature reflection, tempered by long years of conflict and sometimes misunderstanding, was that in the incarnation the Son took into personal union a human nature that from the moment of conception was his own. That humanity has no independent existence by itself; it was and always is the humanity of the Son of God. Therefore, we cannot divide the person of Christ.

On the other hand, his humanity remains humanity and must not be confused with his deity even while it exists solely as the humanity of God the Son. Underlying all this is *both* the Creator-creature distinction, which is inviolate, *and also* the compatibility of God and man, both features we saw to exist in the creation of man.

Moreover, by being solely the humanity of the eternal Son of God, Christ's flesh and soul is permeated with the glorious qualities of the Son, accommodated to human compass. This is what the Eastern church has called *deification*. Christ's human nature was deified by its assumption by the Son of God. It is obvious that this in no way was ever held to jeopardize its integrity as *human* nature. The compatibility of man as created with God underlies this idea.

In Terms of the History of Redemption: The Central Covenant Promise Is Fulfilled in Christ

We now turn to the history of redemption to see how God's covenantal promises focus in the incarnate Christ. In this way Christ's union with us in the incarnation serves as the foundation for all that follows in salvation and, more than that, is at the heart of what salvation involves.

The central promise of God's covenants is the repeated statement in each covenantal administration, "I will be your God; you shall be my people." It is seen in Genesis 17:7–8 in the Abrahamic covenant, in Jeremiah 11:4 in connection with the Mosaic covenant, in Jeremiah 24:7 with the return from Babylonian exile in view, and in Jeremiah 30:22; 31:33; and 32:38 pointing forward to the new covenant. It features also in Revelation 21:3 in the vision of the glorious bride of Christ. This is the heart of all of God's covenants, the promise of God and his people at one in covenant fellowship.

All these promises come to a head in Jesus Christ, who fulfills all of God's covenants. *God is our God in Jesus Christ.* This is abundantly clear in the Gospels, particularly in John. There Jesus Christ is portrayed as the Son of God, Creator and Judge of the world, distinct from the Father but equal to him, of one being with him, and preexisting the creation of the universe. Since Christ is one with God from eternity, he is the definitive and final revelation of God (Heb. 1:1–4). All of God's covenant promises come to fulfillment and fruition in Jesus Christ.

This reminds us of a moving incident reported by Thomas F. Torrance during his service as an army chaplain in Italy during the Second World War. One day, in the heat of battle, Torrance came across a soldier on the point of death.

> As I knelt down and bent over him, he said: "Padre, is God really like Jesus?" I assured him that he was—the only God that there is, the God who had come to us in Jesus, shown his face to us, and poured out his love to us as our Saviour. As I prayed and commended him to the Lord Jesus, he passed away.[66]

God is exactly like Jesus, since Jesus is identical with God.

Furthermore, not only is God our God in Christ, but *in Christ we are God's people*—He is the One who perfectly replies as man to God in faith and obedience. We cannot be God's people in ourselves, since we are by nature sinners and deserving of God's wrath. Thus, our election before the foundation of the world is *in Christ*, and so our whole salvation is *in Christ*, too. It is here that Christ's work as our Great High Priest fits into the picture. In becoming man, he took our place and bore our sins in his body on the tree, rising for our justification and ascending in our flesh to the right hand of the Father. Thus, all of God's historical covenants are centered in Christ and fulfilled by him.[67] Moreover, they are centered in union with Christ—it is in union with him that he is our God and we are his people.

Indeed, the Christian faith can be summed up as, inter alia, a series of unions. There is the union of the three persons in the Trinity, the union of the Son of God with our human nature, the union of Christ with his church, the union established by the Holy Spirit with us as he indwells us. Each of these unions preserves the integrity of the constituent elements or members, being at once a real union and simultaneously not absorbing the one into

---

66. Alister E. McGrath, *Thomas F. Torrance: An Intellectual Biography* (Edinburgh: T&T Clark, 1999), 73–74.
67. Letham, *The Work of Christ*, 39–49.

the other. In his *Hexaemeron*, Robert Grosseteste, bishop of Lincoln from 1230, wrote that at the heart of the Christian faith

> there seem to be grouped together the following unities or unions: the union by which the incarnate Word is the one Christ, one Christ in his person, God and man; the union by which Christ is one in nature with the church through the human nature he took on; and the union by which the church is reunited with him by a condign taking up, in the sacrament of the Eucharist . . . These three unions seem to be grouped together in the One which is called the whole Christ. Of this One the apostle says, to the Ephesians [*sic*]: "For you are all one in Christ Jesus," or, as the Greek text has it: "You are all one person in Christ Jesus." That One of which it says: "That they also may be one in us" seems moreover, to add to the foregoing considerations that the Son, as Word, is one in substance with the Father, and hence with the Holy Spirit . . . It adds also the unity of our conformity in the highest kind with the Blessed Trinity, through our reason. To this conformity and Deiformity we are led by the mediator, Christ, God and man, with whom we form one Christ.

Grosseteste goes on to say that "there is an orderly descent, through the unity of the Trinity and through the incarnate Word, through his body which is the church, to our being one, in a deiform way [or 'one in God-form with the Trinity,' as another possible reading goes]."[68] Grosseteste has put his finger on the pulse of the Christian faith. These unions are the very heartbeat of what God is and all that he has done for us.

Christ Perpetually Has a Human Nature, Body, and Soul

At this present time, Jesus, the Son of God, has ascended to the right hand of the Father and makes perpetual intercession for us. The WLC describes this intercession as his presence before God in our nature. Whether or not he actually prays for us (cf. Luke 22:31–32), any idea of his pleading with an unwilling Father is entirely false; not only are he and the Father one in being, but it is the Father's love that is the source of salvation. Christ's intercession is hardly distinguishable from benediction, the actual bestowal

---

68. *Robert Grosseteste: On the Six Days of Creation: A Translation of the Hexaëmeron*, trans. C. F. J. Martin, Auctores Britannici Medii Aevi (Oxford: Oxford University Press for the British Academy, 1996), 47–48.

of the blessings of salvation, which is his characteristic ministry between the ascension and his return (Luke 24:50–51).[69] It is as the Lamb who has been slain that he appears in the book of Revelation, a perpetual reminder of his humanity, his offering for us on the cross, and his resurrection that followed.

Christ will never divest himself of his assumed humanity, or else we could not be saved. The incarnation is not for the years of time alone but for eternity (WSC 21; WLC 36). This is so because as our Savior he is also the head of his church and will continue to be so without end. Moreover, as the Mediator of creation, he has assumed the full authority given to man in creation, lost and misused by Adam but now fulfilled in his ministry as the second Adam. The Letter to the Hebrews reflects on the poetic description of creation and the task God gave to Adam, in Psalm 8, and sees it realized in the risen and ascended Christ, something that is not conceived as having a terminus. We reflected on that concept in the previous chapter.[70]

It is here that Calvin lapses. In his commentary on 1 Corinthians 15:27, he betrays an almost Nestorian division of the person of Christ and suggests that the assumed humanity may be discarded:

> But Christ will then hand back the Kingdom which he has received, so that we may cleave completely to God. This does not mean that he will abdicate from the Kingdom in this way, but will transfer it in some way or other [*quodammodo*] from his humanity to his glorious divinity, because then there will open up for us a way of approach, from which we are now kept back by our weakness. In this way, therefore, Christ will be subjected to the Father, because, when the veil has been removed, we will see God plainly, reigning in his majesty, and the humanity of Christ will no longer be in between us to hold us back from a nearer vision of God.[71]

This seems to be connected with what Calvin says in the *Institutes*:

> Until he comes forth as judge of the world Christ will therefore reign, joining us to the Father as the measure of our weakness permits. But when as partakers in heavenly glory we shall see God as he is, Christ, having then

---

69. Letham, *The Work of Christ*, 155–57.

70. Correlative with this is the statement in the Niceno-Constantinopolitan creed that Christ's kingdom will never end, aimed at Marcellus of Ancyra, who taught that it was a temporary expedient that would conclude at the final judgment.

71. John Calvin, *Calvin's Commentaries: The First Epistle of Paul the Apostle to the Corinthians*, ed. Thomas F. Torrance and David W. Torrance, trans. John W. Fraser (Grand Rapids: Eerdmans, 1960), 327.

discharged the office of mediator, will cease to be the ambassador of his Father, and will be satisfied with that glory which he enjoyed before the creation of the world.[72]

In the context, Calvin stresses the unity of Christ's person and opposes the Nestorian heresy, so we can only conclude that his comments here are unfortunately clumsy. Instead of seeing Christ's mediatorial kingdom as under the rule of his *person*, it seems that Calvin has placed it under his *human nature*. Since Christ's humanity has no existence of its own, this statement has a worryingly Nestorian ring to it. Moreover, Calvin considers that Christ's humanity prevents us from having close union with God; the whole force of Scripture suggests that it is the *means* by which we know God. Third comes a comment that suggests that Christ's humanity will at least fade from view so as to enable us to draw close to the Father. Beyond this is the hint that Christ will be subordinated to the Father, subjected in such a way that he will no longer hinder us or "hold us back from a nearer vision of God."

Summary

Christ has completely identified himself with us. He is one with us. He everlastingly took our nature into personal union. He is at the Father's right hand in our flesh. In the words of Bishop Christopher Wordworth's hymn "See, the Conqueror Mounts in Triumph":

> You have raised our human nature, in the clouds to God's right hand;
> There we sit, in heavenly places, there with you in glory stand;
> Jesus reigns, adored by angels, man with God is on the throne;
> Mighty Lord, in your ascension we by faith behold our own.

The incarnation is the indispensable basis for union with Christ. Since Christ has united himself to us in the incarnation, we can be united to him by the Holy Spirit.

In itself, the incarnation of the Son of God does not unite us to him, for by itself it does not accomplish salvation. Christ united to himself a human nature, not the nature of the elect—as though the elect had a humanity different from the rest of the human race. Christ's becoming man was to the

---

72. *Institutes*, 2.14.3.

end that he make complete and effective atonement for our sins on the cross, defeat death by his resurrection, and ascend in our nature to the right hand of God. There is no incarnation without atonement.

On the other hand, there can be no atonement without incarnation. It was necessary, according to the just nature of God and on the basis of his eternal decree, that the expiatory and propitiatory death of the Son of God should occur to put away sin once for all. He needed to do this *as man*, for man had sinned in the first place. It was *in our nature* that he offered himself to the Father on the cross, and *in our nature* that he ascended far above all things created, and *in our nature* that he lives and reigns forever—in indissoluble personal union. Therefore, *the incarnation is more than the basis for this union*, as though the union were something else, separable and inherently disconnected. The complete identification of the eternal Son with our flesh and blood is part of our union with him.

Christ's union with us in the incarnation is the foundation for our union with him, both now and in the eternal future. It is a pledge of our sonship, as Calvin wrote, for "our common nature with Christ is the pledge of our fellowship with the Son of God; and clothed with our flesh he vanquished death and sin together that the victory and triumph might be ours. He offered as a sacrifice the flesh he received from us, that he might wipe out our guilt by his act of expiation and appease the Father's righteous wrath."[73] While it is, as Calvin recognized, a weak union in the sense that it is not by itself redemptive,[74] it is central to redemption, not merely as its sine qua non but also because our redemption takes place in Christ, as we will consider in the following chapters.

So the incarnation should not be seen as merely a *means* to salvation. Rather, salvation finds its ultimate fulfillment in the union of humanity with God seen in the incarnate Christ. If, from one angle, the incarnation was the means to atonement and all that followed it, from another (more lasting) perspective, the atonement was the means to the elevation and fruition of humanity in the renewed cosmos over which Christ rules, and we in him.[75]

---

73. Ibid., 2.12.3.

74. Ibid., 3.1.1; *CO*, 15:722–74.

75. See Chul Won Suh, *The Creation Mediatorship of Jesus Christ* (Amsterdam: Rodopi, 1982), for a detailed discussion of the debate as to whether salvation is primarily redemption from sin or else the elevation of the human race to a higher plane, what Dr. Suh terms "restitution-line theology" and "elevation-line theology," respectively. It seems to me that this is a false dilemma.

Yet something more was needed. By this we do not mean something alien to the incarnation as a separable event, an action or a reality disconnected with the Son's assumption of humanity. What we mean is certainly something distinct from the incarnation; it is not the same thing repeated in a different context. But it is inseparable from it, part of the great movement of the grace of the Holy Trinity for us and our salvation. The Son became incarnate, sent by the Father, conceived by the Holy Spirit. This second movement of God's grace consists of the coming of the Holy Spirit at Pentecost, who—proceeding from the Father—is sent by the Son upon his ascension to the Father's right hand.

Tony Lane presents a vivid analogy: electricity lines may go past a house, but to benefit from the electricity supply, the house must be connected to the lines.[76] Many Amish houses in Lancaster County, Pennsylvania do not have electricity, for the strict Amish refuse to introduce it into their homes. Since electricity is carried overhead in that part of the world, as one travels past their houses one can see that they are not connected to the grid and so cannot benefit from the heat and light that it generates. To be united to Christ, we need to be connected to Christ by the Holy Spirit through faith.

> First, we must understand that as long as Christ remains outside of us, and we are separated from him, all that he has suffered and done for the salvation of the human race remains useless and of no value for us.[77]

There are two linked realities here. Without the electricity surging through the grid, the house could have no benefit, even if the wires were connected. If Christ were not incarnate and had not, in our flesh, rendered satisfaction to God's justice on the cross, there would be nothing to deliver us from sin and the just and holy wrath of God. It is in addition to this that the linkage to the grid is possible. Following the sentence cited above, Calvin states:

> Therefore, to share with us what he has received from the Father, he had to become ours and to dwell within us. For this reason, he is called "our Head" [Eph. 4:15], and "the first-born among many brethren" [Rom. 8:29]. We also, in turn, are said to be "engrafted into him" [Rom. 11:17], and "to put

---

76. Anthony N. S. Lane, *Justification by Faith in Catholic-Protestant Dialogue: An Evangelical Assessment* (London: T&T Clark, 2002), 23.
77. *Institutes*, 3.1.1.

on Christ" [Gal. 3:27]; for, as I have said, all that he possesses is nothing to us until we grow into one body with him. It is true that we obtain this by faith. Yet since we see that not all indiscriminately embrace that communion with Christ which is offered in the gospel, reason itself teaches us to climb higher and to examine into the secret energy of the Spirit, by which we come to enjoy Christ and all his benefits.[78]

Both the incarnate Son and the Holy Spirit together, distinctly but indivisibly, bring about our union with Christ. It is the work of the Holy Spirit in uniting us to Christ that we will consider in the next chapter.

---

78. Ibid.

Pentecost

Herman Bavinck points us in the direction we are heading when he writes, "After creation and the incarnation, the outpouring of the Holy Spirit is the third great work of God."[1] The Holy Spirit, who proceeds from the Father and is sent by the Son, is the eternal God, but to a great extent is anonymous as far as we are concerned. This is so because we are material beings and the Spirit is quintessentially of a medium alien to our own familiar bodily territory in a way that the Son, since his incarnation, is not.

The Promise of the Holy Spirit

Integral to the promise of the new covenant was the expectation that Yahweh would pour out his Spirit upon all people. This was clearly foretold by Joel:

> And it shall come to pass afterward, that I will pour out my Spirit on all flesh. (Joel 2:28)

In this way the promise of the new covenant would be fulfilled in which Yahweh declared that he would put his laws not on external tablets but in the hearts of his people (Jer. 31:33). Ezekiel foretells that Yahweh would give his people a heart of flesh instead of a heart of stone:

1. Herman Bavinck, *Reformed Dogmatics*, vol. 3, *Sin and Salvation in Christ* (Grand Rapids: Baker Academic, 2006), 500.

And I will put my Spirit within you, and cause you to walk in my statutes and be careful to obey my rules. (Ezek. 36:27)

The context in which Ezekiel found himself, in exile, was the unbelief and idolatry of Israel that had led Yahweh to impose the sanctions of the Mosaic covenant and to throw the people out of the land. Entailed in this promise is that God's people would believe and obey his word in the future.

The Abrahamic covenant had from the start a universal reach—Abraham was told that in his offspring all the nations of the earth would be blessed (Gen. 12:1–3). In the NT this comes to fruition in the work of the Holy Spirit: first in the life and ministry of the incarnate Son and then in the sending of the Spirit at Pentecost. The result is that the church has "every spiritual blessing in Christ" (Eph. 1:3).

The Holy Spirit in the Life and Ministry of Jesus

Luke highlights the Holy Spirit's activity in the conception and life of Jesus. Boris Bobrinskoy comments about "an exceptional convergence between the outpouring of the Spirit and the birth of Christ."[2] The child is conceived by the Spirit in a manner analogous to his brooding over the waters of creation (Luke 1:34–35; cf. Gen. 1:2); a new creation is brought into being. As God's sovereign power was active in creation, so in salvation a new work of might and irresistible creative force is unleashed by the Holy Spirit. The Spirit is "the One in whom and through whom the Word of God breaks into history."[3] Here is a dramatic lesson that human power cannot save. Thereafter in Luke, every stage of Jesus' infancy and entrance into public ministry is seen in the light of the presence, direction, and empowerment of the Holy Spirit. When Mary visits her cousin, Elizabeth is filled with the Holy Spirit and her baby leaps for joy in her womb (Luke 1:41–44). Elizabeth's husband, Zechariah, is filled with the Holy Spirit when he prophesies concerning his son, John the Baptist (1:67ff.). After the birth of Jesus, when his parents take him to the temple for the ritual of purification, Simeon receives them, and the Holy Spirit was upon him. Simeon had been informed in advance by the Spirit that

2. Boris Bobrinskoy, *The Mystery of the Trinity: Trinitarian Experience and Vision in the Biblical and Patristic Tradition*, trans. Anthony P. Gythiel (Crestwood, NY: St. Vladimir's Seminary Press, 1999), 87.
3. Ibid.

he would see the Christ in person, and on that day, he entered the temple "in the Spirit" (2:25–28).

Later, at the outset of Jesus' public ministry, the Holy Spirit pervades all that happens. John the Baptist's ministry includes, inter alia, announcing that the One who was to come would baptize "with the Holy Spirit and with fire" (Luke 3:16). At Jesus' baptism the Spirit descends on him in the form of a dove (Luke 3:22 and parallels; John 1:32–33). Bobrinskoy calls this "a revelation of the eternal movement of the Spirit of the Father who remains in the Son from all eternity," the Savior's entire life being defined "in a constant, existential relation with the Father in the Spirit."[4] It manifests the eternal resting of the Spirit on the Son.[5] Jesus returns from the Jordan "full of the Holy Spirit," and in turn he is led by the Spirit into the wilderness to be tempted by the devil (Luke 4:1). After this great ordeal, which nevertheless was under the direction of the Spirit of God, Jesus returns to the public sphere, to Galilee, "in the power of the Spirit" (4:14). There in the synagogue he reads from the prophet Isaiah, where he refers to the Spirit of the Lord resting on the Messiah for his work (4:17ff.), declaring that this is now fulfilled in himself. And so on and so forth—in all this Luke informs his readers that Jesus was governed and directed by the Holy Spirit in all that he did. His ministry as the Christ, the Anointed One, was empowered by the Spirit. Behind that, Jesus from his earliest days was in all his human development (cf. 2:40–52) under the immediate leading of the Spirit.

As Bavinck puts it:

> At this point it is important to note that this activity of the Holy Spirit with respect to Christ's human nature absolutely does not stand by itself. Though it began with the conception, it did not stop there. It continued throughout his entire life, even right into the state of exaltation. Generally speaking, the necessity of this activity can be inferred already from the fact that the Holy Spirit is the author of all creaturely life and specifically of the religious-ethical life in humans. The true human who bears God's image is inconceivable even for a moment without the indwelling of the Holy Spirit.[6]

4. Ibid., 88, 91.
5. Ibid., 94, 99.
6. Bavinck, *Reformed Dogmatics*, 3:292.

The Holy Spirit Comes at Pentecost to Indwell Countless Human Persons, Uniting Them to Christ

A central theme in the Upper Room Discourse, recorded in John 14–17, is the sending of the Holy Spirit at Pentecost. Jesus was to depart. But he would not leave his disciples alone as orphans. He would come to them in the person of the *paraklētos*. His sending was to follow Jesus' resurrection and ascension. This is clear in Jesus' own pronouncement in John 7:37–39 and John's explanatory comment; the Spirit was not yet given, since Jesus had not yet been glorified. It is why Jesus' remarks in the upper room are all couched in the future tense.

The Holy Spirit was sent by Jesus after his glorification. This is the message Peter conveyed on the day of Pentecost in explaining the amazing phenomena that happened that day:

> This Jesus God raised up, and of that we are all witnesses. Being therefore exalted at the right hand of God, and having received from the Father the promise of the Holy Spirit, he has poured out this that you yourselves are seeing and hearing. (Acts 2:32–33 ESV)

In the upper room, Jesus explained the ministry of the Spirit. He would lead the apostles into all truth, those things that Jesus himself had not taught at that time because they were unable to understand and appreciate them (John 16:12–15). He would principally testify about Christ, not drawing attention to himself (vv. 13–14). He was to convince the world of sin, righteousness, and judgment (vv. 8–11).

Above all, the Spirit would come to indwell believers and unite them to Christ (John 14:16–23). Jesus had already taught his disciples of his own identity, while distinct, with the Father. He and God are coordinate objects of faith (14:1). Whoever has seen him has seen the Father (vv. 8–10). This is because he and the Father indwell each other.

> Do you not believe that I am in the Father and the Father is in me? The words that I say to you I do not speak on my own authority, but the Father who dwells in me does his works. Believe me that I am in the Father and the Father is in me. (John 14:10–11 ESV)

This is a reference to what in Trinitarian theology is termed the *perichorēsis*, the mutual indwelling of the three Trinitarian persons. In the words of Gerald

Bray, the persons occupy the same infinite divine space.[7] The Father and the Son are both fully God. All that can be said to be God is possessed by both. Yet they are distinct. The Father and the Son—and, by extension, the Spirit—are *in* each other in indissoluble union. This union does not infringe the distinctness of either.

Jesus goes on to say that when the Spirit comes, he will indwell his disciples. Moreover, they will then know for themselves that he and the Father are in each other. On top of this, they will also know that Christ is in them, presumably by the Holy Spirit.

"In that day you will know that I am in my Father, and you in me, and I in you" (v. 20). There is a pattern here, an analogy, between the indwelling of the Father and the Son on the one hand and the indwelling of Christ and his disciples on the other. There is an obvious difference; the Father and the Son are one in being, eternal, immense, while Christ and his multitudinous disciples are distinguishably separate. The context points to the Holy Spirit as the agent of the indwelling. He indwells countless people, who remain individuals although relational individuals, individuals in communion, in union with God the Spirit, indwelt by him.

Further on, Jesus enlarges on what he has just said. In verse 23, having affirmed that the one who loves him will be loved by him and his Father, Jesus adds:

> If anyone loves me, he will keep my word, and my Father will love him, and we will come to him and make our home with him. (ESV)

Here both the Father and the Son will come to the one who loves Jesus. Once again, the context points to the activity of the promised Holy Spirit. In the coming of the Spirit to indwell, the Father and the Son are also indivisibly present. The loving disciple will have intimate communion and union with the whole Trinity, in the person of the Holy Spirit. Behind this lies the fact that all three persons operate together indivisibly in all the works of God, yet each work is specifically attributable to one of them. Thus the Son died on the cross, while offering himself to the Father by the eternal Spirit (Heb. 9:14). So here, the Holy Spirit—neither the Father nor the Son—was sent at Pentecost, yet he was sent by the Father in or through the Son. Consequently, in the indwelling of the Spirit, the Father and the Son are also inseparably

7. Gerald L. Bray, *The Doctrine of God* (Leicester, UK: Inter-Varsity Press, 1993), 158.

involved.[8] This is no merely ephemeral thing. The Spirit is not a temporary visitor. Jesus insists that he and the Father will make their permanent
residence with this one. *Monē* denotes a permanent dwelling, in contrast to
a short-term expedient such as a tent. This great event occurred on the day
of Pentecost, recorded by Luke in Acts 2, but the result is permanent.

Paul reflects on themes such as these in 1 Corinthians 12:12–13, where
he addresses questions arising from the Spirit's ministry in the church there:

> For just as the body is one and has many members, and all the members of
> the body, though many, are one body, so it is with Christ. For in one Spirit
> we were all baptized into one body—Jews or Greeks, slaves or free—and
> all were made to drink of one Spirit. (ESV)

In the background here are the sacraments of baptism and the Eucharist.
The Holy Spirit baptizes all believers into one body. The image is of saturation by the Spirit. As a result, we are added to, and united with, the body, in
the pervasive medium of the Spirit himself. As the baptismal water covers
and saturates, so the Holy Spirit permeates.[9] The oneness of the body is the
direct outflow of the enveloping pervasion of the Spirit. Moreover, there is a
reciprocal and responsive action on our part, which in turn depends on the
grace of God—we were all given to drink of the one Spirit. This is redolent
of the drinking of Christ's blood in the Lord's Supper, imbibed not corporeally or materially but *in the Holy Spirit.* Again, as surely as we drink, so the
Spirit enters us and saturates us on an ongoing basis, for he has come, with
the Father and the Son, to take up permanent residence within us.

In Galatians 4:4–6, Paul writes of the movement of God to man in the
incarnation, in which God sent his Son "when the time had fully come" (v. 4),
in order to redeem us and to grant us sonship (*exapesteilen ho theos ton huion
autou . . . hina tēn hiuothesian apolabōmen*). This is mirrored by his move-

---

8. Robert Letham, *The Holy Trinity: In Scripture, History, Theology, and Worship* (Phillipsburg, NJ:
P&R Publishing, 2004), 186–93.

9. On dipping as the original mode of baptism, see Hughes Oliphant Old, *The Shaping of the
Reformed Baptismal Rite in the Sixteenth Century* (Grand Rapids: Eerdmans, 1992), 264–82; Robert
Letham, "Baptism in the Writings of the Reformers," *SBET* 7, 2 (Autumn 1989): 21–44; Robert Letham,
The Westminster Assembly: Reading Its Theology in Historical Context (Phillipsburg, NJ: P&R Publishing,
2009), 339–45; Certain Learned Divines, *Annotations upon All the Books of the Old and New Testament;
Wherein the Text Is Explained, Doubts Resolved, Scriptures Paralleled, and Various Readings Observed*
(London: John Legatt and John Raworth, 1645), Wing / 351.01, on Romans 6:4; and from the Orthodox
perspective—and the Greeks certainly know a thing or two about their own language—Timothy Ware,
The Orthodox Church (London: Penguin Books, 1969), 284.

ment to man at Pentecost. Since we are now sons, God has sent the Spirit of his Son "into our hearts" at Pentecost (*exapesteilen ho theos to pneuma tou huiou autou eis tas kardias hēmōn*) (v. 6). Here the Spirit is described as the Spirit of the Son, reminiscent of the unity of the risen Christ and the Holy Spirit to which Paul refers in 2 Corinthians 3:16–17, in calling the Spirit "the Spirit of the Lord." Since the Spirit of the Father's Son indwells us, it follows that he assures us that we are the children of God (1 John 3:24).

Entailed in this is the gift of faith by which we are united to Christ. Paul and John both record that saving faith is the gift of God and that we would be incapable of it without the Holy Spirit's drawing us to Christ. Paul insists that fallen man is "dead in trespasses and sins" (Eph. 2:1) and so unable to effect a change to his dire condition. Jesus taught the disciples that no one can come to him unless the Father draws him; faith is a gift of God (John 6:44–45, 64–65). This, as Calvin put it, is the principal work of the Holy Spirit.[10]

Rowland Stedman wrote that the way in which Christ and his people are united is that "the Lord Christ, by his Spirit, taketh possession of them, and dwelleth in them; and Believers through faith of the operation of the Spirit, take hold of Christ, and get into him; and so they are knit together and become one." The Lord Jesus "cometh and taketh up residence in them; and they are inabled to go forth unto Christ, and receive him as he is offered in the Gospel; whereby they are in him: and thus this Union is established."[11] According to Stedman, there are "two great bonds or ligaments" of this union. On Christ's part, he dwells in believers by his Spirit. On their part, they apprehend Christ by faith and "take him home, as it were, unto themselves."[12] The first is what Stedman calls a natural bond, while the second he terms a legal bond. The natural bond is the same as the positive element of regeneration. It is total, Christ taking possession of the whole person. It is beyond human power to effect this, although we are required to attend the means of grace for it to happen.[13] By this "our natures are fashioned according to his nature," since there is "a suitableness" between Christ's human nature and that of a person being

---

10. *Institutes*, 3.1.1.

11. Rowland Stedman, *The Mystical Union of Believers with Christ, or A Treatise Wherein That Great Mystery and Priviledge of the Saints Union with the Son of God Is Opened* (London: W. R. for Thomas Parkhurst, at the Golden-Bible on London-Bridge, under the gate, 1668), 121, Wing / 335:13.

12. Ibid., 122.

13. Ibid., 123–32.

sanctified.[14] We will explore the ramifications of this in the next two chapters. In legal terms, the union is akin to that of a debtor and a surety, for "the law reckoneth them as one." The payment made by the surety is accounted as if the debtor had paid it himself because of the oneness that exists between them in the eyes of the law.[15] We will discuss this aspect in detail in chapter 4. Stedman further points to what he calls a moral union, of which love is the bond, as in the case of intimate friends. In this sense, "so are the Lord Jesus and his peculiar people knit together." He dwells in them and they, in turn, hunger and thirst after further enjoyment of him.[16] There may be a hint here of the emergence of the dangers of a separation between the imputational and transformative to which Evans points.[17]

Christ Sharing Our Nature, We by Grace Are United to Him, according to His Humanity

We have argued in this chapter that the Holy Spirit is the One who brings about our union with Christ in our life history. He does this by grace through faith. Our faith and all that flows from it in the Christian life is due to the Holy Spirit, who renews us in the image of God—which is Christ—and transforms us continually into Christ (2 Cor. 3:18). Eventually, when Christ returns in glory, we will be like him (1 John 3:1–2). This entire amazing process occurs through faith, which is the way we receive Christ. Therefore, we come empty, with nothing to offer. Saving faith, as WCF 14.2 describes it, is principally "receiving, and resting upon Christ alone for salvation." As Lane remarks, in connection with Calvin and the Reformers, "faith is effective not in itself but because it unites us to Christ. Justification is by faith alone not because of what faith merits or *achieves* but because of what it *receives*."[18]

Faith is "the principal work of the Holy Spirit," as we saw that Calvin said. The Spirit unites us to Christ. As a house benefits from electricity when hooked up to the grid, so we benefit from the work of Christ when

14. Ibid., 133.

15. Ibid., 134–35.

16. Ibid., 148–49.

17. See William B. Evans, *Imputation and Impartation: Union with Christ in American Reformed Theology* (Eugene, OR: Wipf & Stock, 2008). I am indebted to Bill Evans himself for this observation.

18. Anthony N. S. Lane, *Justification by Faith in Catholic-Protestant Dialogue: An Evangelical Assessment* (London: T&T Clark, 2002), 26.

it becomes ours by our being in union with him. In this, not only is he our substitute and representative, acting in our place and on our behalf, but we are one with him. His work is ours because we are on the same team. If, in a game of soccer, the goalkeeper makes a massive blunder and lets in the decisive goal at the last minute, the whole team loses the game. Conversely, if the striker, with seconds left, scores a brilliant goal to win the game 3–2, the whole team participates in the victory. In a similar way, Christ has made atonement and won the victory for his team, while in turn the Holy Spirit selects us for his team. There the analogy stops, for in this case, the Spirit achieves this by being poured into our hearts and bringing about a relationship much closer than can ever be envisioned in a sports team.

We Thereby Share Christ's Relation to the Father

Since we are united to Christ, God regards us in the identical way he does Christ. The Father treats us in exactly the same way as he does his own eternal and beloved Son.

Jesus consistently described himself as God's Son. In turn, he called God his Father. He used this term not as a simile (God is *like* a father), nor even as a metaphor (using the word in an unusual way in order to highlight aspects of his character that might otherwise pass unnnoticed). Instead, he regarded it as his personal name; this is the proper way to address God. This is in stark contrast to the image of God as a mother, which is used as a simile on occasion in the OT but never as a metaphor and does not recur at all in the NT.

This was revolutionary. No Jew would think of speaking of God like this. Indeed, Jesus' opponents accused him of blasphemy and took up stones to stone him. Jesus' defense was not that he had been misunderstood but that he was innocent of blasphemy, since he was telling the truth. In each case, he proceeds to reinforce his claims and takes them one stage further. From claiming equality with God (John 5:16–47) he asserts identity with God the Father (10:22–36) and places himself as coordinate with God as the object of faith (14:1), because whoever has seen him has seen the Father also, since they indwell one another (14:7–11).

Because of this, and the fact that we are united with Christ, we, too, can call God "our Father." Jesus taught his disciples to pray, "Our Father . . .

in heaven." This is to be the customary way to pray. It entails adoption as sons and continuing sonship thereafter (Matt. 6:9; Luke 11:2). It is a sharing in the unique relation that Jesus has to the Father. He is the Son by nature; we are sons by grace and adoption. As such, we become coheirs with Christ (Rom. 8:15–17). The Holy Spirit, who indwells and saturates us, grants us the knowledge of this sonship (Gal. 4:4–6). In both these instances—Romans 8 and Galatians 4—the Holy Spirit is poured into our hearts and gives us the knowledge of our own adoption as sons, whether we are Jews (*abba*) or Gentiles (*patēr*).[19] We will explore these great matters in more detail in the chapters that follow.

Summary

Let us summarize what we have found so far. Union with Christ rests, in the first place, on God's having created man to be compatible with him on the finite level. He made us for himself. This is correlative with his being the Creator and our being his creatures. In making man in his image, he had the goal of Christ—the image of the invisible God—becoming man, and man's being united to him.

Second, union with Christ is based on the foundation of Christ's union with us in his incarnation. He, the eternal Son of the Father, of the identical being as the Father, took human nature into personal union. He then and now has a human body and soul. He became one of us while remaining who he always was and is. This is a personal—hypostatic—union. The *person* of the Son unites to himself a single human nature.

Third, Christ, the eternal Son, having united human nature in himself, now unites us with himself by the Holy Spirit, as the Spirit draws us to him in faith. This is not a personal union, as we saw in the incarnation of the Son. In this case, the Holy Spirit enters, indwells, saturates, and pervades countless human persons and so brings them into union with Christ the Son. As the Puritan John Flavel put it, in reflecting on John 17:23, para-

---

19. The current tendency, influenced by the pressure of gender-inclusive language, to refer to believers as "sons and daughters" of God is misleading, blurs this vital truth, and has the effect of blunting the church's appreciation of what union with Christ entails. Jesus Christ is the Son of the Father, and is so eternally; that is his name and that is his status. It is not a sexual term, for God is not a sexual being. By referring to Christian believers as "sons," the NT is not, under the influence of patriarchal culture, bypassing half the human race. Instead, it is pointing to our shared status with the Son of the Father, in and by the Holy Spirit. The introduction of talk of "daughters" obscures this point, placed at the hub of the Christian life.

phrasing Jesus' words: "Here is the mystical union betwixt Christ and the saints, *q.d.* Thou and I are one essentially, they and I are one mystically: and thou and I are one by communication of the Godhead, and singular fulness of the Spirit to me as Mediator: and they and I are one, by my communication of the Spirit to them in measure."[20]

The question remains: of what does this union with Christ consist? We will attempt to explore this question, insofar as we are able, in the following chapters.

---

20. *The Works of John Flavel* (London: Banner of Truth, 1968), 2:34.

Union with Christ and Representation

Christ Represents Us because He Is Our Covenant Head

There is a legal aspect to union with Christ. God is just. From the first, he required of Adam obedience to his law as a means to being confirmed in a righteous relationship with himself and to receiving life (Gen. 2:15–17). After the fall his law was, and is, the standard by which our obligations in the covenant of grace are to be measured. Consequently, salvation in Christ is founded on a legal, forensic base. For example, the first thing of significance in the atonement was that God might be just (Rom. 3:26).

In this, Christ fulfilled the law on our behalf, as our representative. He did this in what is termed his *active obedience*—his obedience as man to the demands of God's holy law. Adam when created was responsible to obey the laws of God. He failed to do this, breaking the command not to eat of the fruit of the tree of the knowledge of good and evil. Adam was a public person, acting not for himself alone but for the whole race in solidarity with him. As a result, not only was his guilt his own, but all people shared in it. Adam and the whole race were also plunged into a state of corruption, and placed under the condemnation of God. Paul makes this clear in Romans 5:12–21, where he draws a comparison between Adam and his sin, which brought death and condemnation, and Christ's obedience, which brings justification and life. Moreover, in 1 Corinthians 15:20–23, Paul again places Adam and Christ in contrast: the one brought death to all; the other brings life and resurrection.

This is part of a theme of corporate solidarity seen throughout Scripture. When one man—Achan—sinned, all Israel sinned (Josh. 7:1–26). Individuals are not identified in isolation; they are A the son of B the son of C of the tribe of D. There is a certain similarity to a team: if the captain of the team scores a goal against his own team in the last minute, the whole team loses. In this case, the captain represents the team, his actions implicating the whole. At the same time, he is one with the team. What he does is the doing of the team in his own person. This thinking is alien to the modern Western mind-set, governed as it is by the individualism of the Renaissance and Enlightenment. We speak of one man, one vote. Each person must decide for himself or herself.

Christ, in his incarnate life and ministry, was the second Adam. Man had sinned; man must put things right, not only by avoiding sin but by actually rendering to God the obedience that Adam failed to supply. Yet if he were born by the identical procedure as the rest of the race, he would inherit Adam's guilt and the corrupt nature conveyed by natural generation. Moreover, purely as man he would lack the ability to bring about salvation. Therefore, the Son of God stepped in, became incarnate by the Holy Spirit of the virgin Mary, took Adam's place, and obeyed the Father. He did this throughout his life. As man, he was a new creation, the Holy Spirit coming upon Mary, overshadowing her as he did the waters of creation (Luke 1:34–35; cf. Gen. 1:2). He was captain of a new team, head of the new humanity the Father had given him before the foundation of the world.

So the young Jesus grew in favor with God and man (Luke 2:52). He progressed from one degree of obedience to another; the incident at the temple on his twelfth birthday was an example of immature obedience, following the work his Father had given him.[1] Later, he issued a confident challenge to his opponents to convict him of sin (John 8:46); not only could they not do so, but in itself the challenge disclosed his having a clear conscience. The NT consistently witnesses to his sinlessness. At the same time, it asserts in no uncertain terms his true humanity—hunger and thirst, weariness and sorrow, friendships and grief at bereavement, responsibilities to his mother, temptation, sufferings, death, and burial. He wholeheartedly obeyed the law of God (John 4:34; 17:4). Even when faced with the imminent death planned from eternity and the possibility of evading it (Matt. 26:39; Heb. 10:7), he did not turn aside, for it was necessary to repair the

---

1. Robert Letham, *The Work of Christ* (Leicester, UK: Inter-Varsity Press, 1993), 113–14.

damage caused by the first Adam (Rom. 5:12–21). This is termed his *active obedience*, his positive fulfilling of the law of God, on our behalf and in our place but also in union with us. He did this not merely externally to us—instead of us, like a substitute. Because of his union with us and our union with him, we were in him as he did it. He was captain of the team, and his actions are ours.

Moreover, there was another aspect to his obedience to the Father, his *passive obedience* (from *patior*, "to suffer"), by which he underwent for us the penalty of the broken law. We had sinned in Adam, death and condemnation the result. In order for us to be restored to God's favor, at the very least (for salvation, as we will see, means far more than that) the penalty of that broken law had to be suffered in Christ.[2] Hence the NT witness to Christ suffering, "the just for the unjust to bring us to God" (1 Peter 3:18; cf. Rom. 3:25; 4:25; 5:8; Heb. 10:1–14; 1 Peter 2:21f.). So he gave his life a ransom for many (Matt. 20:28; Mark 10:45). By his obedience the many are declared righteous (Rom. 5:12–21). These two aspects of Christ's obedience in reality are parts of his whole united obedience to God.[3]

Christ Represents Us because He Shares Our Nature

Christ is perfectly qualified to be our representative for two overwhelming reasons. First, he is the eternal Son of God. In Hebrews 4:14–16, the author writes of "Jesus the Son of God who has passed through the heavens." This is a reference to his identity as the Son of God, supreme over the prophets, angels, Moses, and the OT priesthood, and also to his ascension to the right hand of the Father, a recurring theme throughout the letter. It demonstrates that he is *able* to help us in time of need because of who he is (the Son of God) and what he has done (ascended to the position of supreme authority). Second, he has taken our nature into union, and so he is absolutely *qualified* to be our representative. He was "tested in all points as we are, yet without sin." He can help us because he has experienced temptation and resisted it implacably. In his incarnation he took into union our human nature. All that he is and all that he did and does for us as our Mediator is in our nature. His human obedience is vicarious throughout, from his temptation as the second

---

2. The alternative is to bear that penalty ourselves, eternal death and condemnation, bearing the just and holy wrath of God.

3. Letham, *The Work of Christ*, 113–21.

Adam (Matt. 4:1–10) up to his resurrection (1 Cor. 15:22) and ascension (Eph. 2:6ff.).[4] In the words of the fifteenth-century Latin hymn:

> O love, how deep, how broad, how high! How passing thought and fantasy,
> That God, the Son of God, should take our mortal form for mortals' sake.
>
> For us baptized, for us he bore his holy fast, and hungered sore;
> For us temptations sharp he knew, for us the tempter overthrew.
>
> For us to wicked men betrayed, scourged, mocked, in crown of thorns arrayed;
> For us he bore the cross's death, for us at length gave up his breath.
>
> For us he rose from death again, for us he went on high to reign;
> For us he sent his Spirit here to guide, to strengthen, and to cheer.

Since the Spirit unites us to Christ through faith, Christ's substitutionary and representative work is effected for us and consequently in us.

Union with Christ and the Atonement

Christ Is Our Substitute

Jesus took our place throughout his life and ministry and especially on the cross and in his resurrection and ascension. A substitute takes the place occupied by someone else; in a soccer match, the substitute comes onto the pitch and replaces another player, who leaves the game at the same time. The NT is full of language that speaks of Christ in this way. Its particular focus is on the cross, on his atoning sacrifice made there for sinners.

The Gospels record Jesus' words at the Last Supper (Luke 22:19 and parallels), and Paul repeats them (1 Cor. 11:24). Jesus, on the night in which he was betrayed, said, "This is my body, which is for you," and "this is my blood of the covenant, which is poured out for many for the remission of sins [*to peri pollōn ekchunnomenon*]" (Matt. 26:26–29). This follows his claim that he "did not come to be served but to serve, and to give his life a ransom for many [*lutron anti pollōn*]" (Matt. 20:28; Mark 10:45). Jesus described his

---

4. Ibid., 116f.

impending death as given "for the life of the world [*huper tēs tou kosmou zōēs*]" (John 6:51). Caiaphas's unknowing and ironic prophecy that Jesus was to die on behalf of the nation runs along similar lines, in its pointing to the benefit of one man's dying instead of the whole nation (John 11:50).

Paul characteristically writes of the atonement in substitutionary terms. The central theme of the gospel is that "Christ died for our sins [*huper tōn hamartiōn hēmōn*] according to the Scriptures" (1 Cor. 15:3). Paul reiterates this in his second letter to Corinth when he says that "one died for all [*heis huper pantōn apethanen*]" (2 Cor. 5:14–15), leading to his most profound claim that "he who knew no sin was made sin for us that we might become the righteousness of God in him" (2 Cor. 5:21). Elsewhere he asserts that Christ died for us (*Christos huper hēmōn apethanen* [Rom. 5:8]), that the Father gave up his Son for us all (Rom. 8:32), and that Christ gave his life a ransom for all (1 Tim. 2:6).

Peter has the same doctrine as Paul. Christ bore our sins in his own body on the tree (1 Peter 2:21–24). He died, the just for the unjust (1 Peter 3:18). The *author of Hebrews* states that he was once offered to bear the sins of many (Heb. 9:28). Behind all these statements—which are merely representative samples—lies the OT sacrificial ritual in Leviticus 4–5, in which a man offered an animal sacrifice; the pronouncement "he is guilty" was followed by the sprinkling of the altar with the blood of the slain animal and the declaration "he is forgiven." The offerer was symbolically cleared from his sins by the animal's dying instead of him. Clearly, animal sacrifices were inadequate to atone for human sin. They simply foreshadowed the one great sacrifice of Christ on the cross, effective for all time to atone for the sins of his people.[5]

Christ Is Our Representative

All that Jesus did and does is on our behalf. A representative acts on behalf of others. In Britain, a member of Parliament votes on behalf of his constituents, and voices their interests in Parliament. A member of Congress similarly represents the electorate in his district or state. His actions are those of the ones he represents. An ambassador represents his country; his words are understood to reflect the policies of his country's government.[6]

---

5. See Alan M. Stibbs, *The Meaning of the Word "Blood" in Scripture* (London: Tyndale Press, 1948); Leon Morris, *The Apostolic Preaching of the Cross* (London: Tyndale Press, 1955); Letham, *The Work of Christ*, 132–40.

6. This is the constitutional position. Sadly, we know that in many cases members of Congress represent vested interests such as big business or other groups that have financed their election.

In this sense, Paul describes Christ as being handed over for our offenses and raised for our justification (Rom. 4:25). He then explains that Christ was not acting on his own account but was the head and representative of his people. As Adam represented the whole human race and so, when he sinned, he plunged the entire race into sin, misery, and death, so Christ, in his obedience, acted on behalf of his own people (Rom. 5:12–21). As a result, his obedience is reckoned to them, and so they are accounted or constituted righteous. Some of the passages cited above on substitution carry this representative theme as well. Whereas a substitute takes the place of another person, a representative acts on behalf of that person. He is not simply another individual; his actions are to be regarded as those of the ones he represents. This is particularly clear in the case of the high priesthood of Christ, expounded in Hebrews against the backdrop of the OT high priest. There, Aaron entered the Holy of Holies once a year on the Day of Atonement to represent the people of Israel. His high priestly garments indicated this function; the breastplate contained twelve jewels, symbolizing the twelve tribes of Israel. When he entered the sanctuary, he carried these jewels on his person, bringing them before Yahweh, the atoning sacrifice being on behalf of the people. Aaron had already offered sacrifice first for his own sins, for without this preparation he would not be fit to enter the presence of Yahweh on behalf of others. In Christ's case, he had no sins for which to atone, and so he entered heaven at his ascension in his own right, thoroughly equipped to act on behalf of his people (Heb. 4:14–5:10; 6:18–20; 7:23–8:1; 9:11–10:14).

On this basis, Christ, on the cross, took our place and endured the full brunt of the wrath of God for us. Moreover, in doing so, he represented us and in his resurrection and ascension to the right hand of the Father acts on our behalf.

Christ Acts in Union with Us: We Are United to Christ

As both substitute and representative, Christ is seen as distinct from those who benefit from what he did. A substitute is, by definition, another person than the one he replaces. A representative, similarly, acts on behalf of another. While his actions are legally accounted as those of the one he represents, the two are distinctly separate persons. The concept of union takes us a stage further than either of these two metaphors. In this case, all that Christ did and does we do, since we are one with him. The "otherness" of a substitute or representative is in the background. Not only does Christ act in our place as a substitute, and on our behalf as our representative, but because of the union sustained between Christ and ourselves, his actions *are* ours. At the same time, the otherness of the substitute and representative should prevent any thought of our being merged with Christ or undergoing a change of essence.[7]

This is of immense importance when we consider the argument, in connection with the atonement, that it would be unjust for God to acquit the guilty and discharge the innocent. This argument is correct and has strong biblical backing from the OT, and from the character of God. It was a principle enshrined in the civil law of the Mosaic covenant:

> You shall not pervert the justice due to your poor in his lawsuit. Keep far from a false charge, and do not kill the innocent and righteous, for I will not acquit the wicked. And you shall take no bribe, for a bribe blinds the clear-sighted and subverts the cause of those who are in the right. (Ex. 23:6–8)

> "Cursed be anyone who takes a bribe to shed innocent blood." And all the people shall say, "Amen." (Deut. 27:25)

It is reinforced in Proverbs:

> He who justifies the wicked and he who condemns the righteous
>   are both alike an abomination to the LORD. (Prov. 17:15; cf. 24:24)

> To impose a fine on a righteous man is not good. (Prov. 17:26)

> It is not good to be partial to the wicked
>   or to deprive the righteous of justice. (Prov. 18:5)

The prophets pronounce woes on rulers "who acquit the guilty for a bribe, and deprive the innocent of his right" (Isa. 5:23). Underlying this is the justice of Yahweh, who "will by no means clear the guilty" (Ex. 34:7).

The significance of this principle is seen in the book *Pierced for Our Transgressions*. The authors answer dozens of objections to the penal substitutionary doctrine of the atonement, one after the other, most or all of which use this argument, or variations of it, as a basis for their opposition

---

7. See Mark A. Garcia, "Imputation and the Christology of Union with Christ: Calvin, Osiander and the Contemporary Quest for a Reformed Model," *WTJ* 68 (2006): 219–51.

to the doctrine. As soon as one objection is answered, another appears on the scene, and the process is repeated over and over again.[8] Yet these counterarguments are all offset by union with Christ. Once union with Christ is brought to bear on the matter, the scenario changes. It is no longer a case of God's punishing the innocent and letting the guilty off scot-free. Because of the union established between Christ and his elect people, the wrongs done by the guilty parties have become Christ's as well. In turn, the righteousness of the One who bears the punishment actually belongs to the other, since both are regarded as one.

As Hugh Martin wrote, "The possibility of real atonement absolutely postulates and demands a conjunction between him who atones and those for whom his atonement is available. This is beyond need of proof."[9] This is the question that Martin proposes: what kind of conjunction is needed between Christ and the sinner for his redeeming work? His answer: a conjunction that goes beyond his union with us in the incarnation, since that union is with human nature in general and does not of itself benefit any person in particular.[10] Moreover, it goes beyond substitution and representation, for these merely beg the question of how and why Christ is a substitute and representative. It points to what Martin calls the everlasting covenant in which the union of Christ and his people was established. "He is substituted *for us*, because he is one *with us*."[11] He argues that it is a covenant between the Father and the Son. The Westminster Assembly, on the other hand, pointed to a determination between God the Trinity and Christ as second Adam and head of his elect.[12] This latter position has the backing of classic Reformed theology prior to the Assembly. But Martin—as well as others who follow him—equally agrees that union between Christ and his people, established in the eternal counsels of God, underlies the atonement and gives it its meaning.[13] From this it follows that when Christ died on the cross and rose from

---

8. Steve Jeffery, Michael Ovey, and Andrew Sach, *Pierced for Our Transgressions: Recovering the Glory of Penal Substitution* (Wheaton, IL: Crossway, 2007).

9. Hugh Martin, *The Atonement: In Its Relations to the Covenant, the Priesthood, the Intercession of Our Lord* (Edinburgh: Lyon and Gemmell, 1877), 38.

10. Ibid., 40–41.

11. Ibid., 42–44.

12. WLC 31: "Q. With whom was the covenant of grace made? A. The covenant of grace was made with Christ as the second Adam, and in him with all the elect as his seed."

13. Martin verges on tritheism, at least in forms of expression if not intent, when he talks of the will of the Father, the will of the Son, and—by implication—the will of the Holy Spirit. Classic Trinitarian theology has maintained that the three have one will, since will is a predicate of nature rather than person. The three persons act inseparably and indivisibly in all God's ways and works, since the Trinity

the dead, we are really and truly the ones who died and rose with him, as Paul says in Romans 6:1ff. Moreover, it also follows that when he died, our sin was utterly and definitively dealt with, since Christ died in union with us and we with him. Sin can no longer have dominion over us!

The atonement is integrally connected to the doctrine of justification. It remains for us to examine how union with Christ and justification are related. Before we do that, we must backtrack a little. Our investigation of the atonement has led us to reflect on the eternal counsels of the Trinity, the root of our entire salvation, the atonement and justification included. First, then, we will inquire into how union with Christ comes to expression in the eternal decree of election and the loving plan of the Holy Trinity to save us in union with Christ the incarnate Son.

Union with Christ and Election

That election takes place *in Christ* is clear in the NT. Where Paul writes of our being chosen by God, he invariably describes it as in union with Christ. Thus, in Ephesians 1:4 he states that the God and Father of our Lord Jesus Christ "chose us *in him* before the foundation of the world." He attributes election to the God and Father of Christ, affirms that it was an eternal decision that occurred before the universe existed, and states that it was "in him," in Christ. Since in the rest of the paragraph he unfolds the panorama of salvation as occurring in Christ at each and every stage, it follows that it is in union with Christ, the beloved Son, that our eternal election was made. Paul says much the same in 2 Timothy 1:9, where he refers to God's grace, "which he gave us in Christ before the ages began." In the great chain of salvation that Paul unfolds in Romans 8:29–30, God's predestining us was so that we may "be conformed to the image of his Son, in order that he might be the firstborn among many brothers." This echoes the words of Jesus, recorded by John, to the effect that the Father had given him certain people who in the course of time came to him, and whom he would never under any circumstances cast out (John 6:37–40). The doctrine of election cannot be understood biblically and theologically if it is abstracted from its being in Christ. It is a Trinitarian decree, it bears the

---

is indivisible; see Martin, *Atonement*, 45. Perhaps this is why Martin considers God's decrees as cold and unloving. How can that be so, since the Trinity is perfect love and all of God's holy plans and purposes reflect the goodness and love that forever is characteristic of who he is?

closest connection to the person and work of Christ, it cannot be severed from the gospel, and it is the root and foundation of all the other ways in which union with Christ is worked out in human history and in the life experience of the faithful. It is as far from fatalism as could be imagined.[14]

So much is evident when we consider the various expositions of the theme in classic Reformed theology. We will consider a number of representative Reformed theologians and confessions. This is not a claim that the views expressed there were unanimously agreed, but rather that these doctrines are rooted in significant figures in the Reformed tradition.

John Calvin (1509–64)

For Calvin, assurance of election is to be sought in Christ precisely because we were chosen in Christ before the foundation of the world. Any attempt on our part to probe the mysteries of election is in vain, for it is beyond us. Yet God has revealed himself in his Son, in whom we have salvation.

> Accordingly, those whom God has adopted as his sons are said to have been chosen not in themselves but in his Christ [Eph. 1:4] for unless he could love them in him, he could not honor them with the inheritance of his Kingdom if they had not previously become partakers of him. But if we have been chosen in him, we shall not find assurance of our election in ourselves; and not even in God the Father, if we conceive him as severed from his Son. Christ, then, is the mirror wherein we must, and without self-deception may, contemplate our own election. For since it is into his body the Father has destined those to be engrafted whom he has willed from eternity to be his own, that he may hold as sons all whom he acknowledges to be among his members, we have a sufficiently clear and firm testimony that we have been inscribed in the book of life [cf. Rev. 21:27] if we are in communion with Christ.[15]

Calvin considers that election in Christ has definite practical implications. We can have assurance of our election in this life if we are in communion with Christ, since we were elected in union with him. Faith in Christ here and now mirrors the eternal electing purpose of God, since the latter was

---

14. For further discussion, see Letham, *The Work of Christ*, 53–56; Richard A. Muller, *Christ and the Decree: Christology and Predestination in Reformed Theology from Calvin to Perkins* (Grand Rapids: Baker, 1986).

15. *Institutes*, 3.24.5.

undertaken with Christ as our head. Calvin considers that Christ "claims for himself, in common with the Father, the right to choose."[16] Furthermore, following Augustine, he talks of Christ as the first of the elect, since he himself was chosen to the office of Mediator. He is "the clearest light of predestination and grace," appointed Mediator solely by God's good pleasure.[17] The Father has gathered us together in Christ the head and joined us to himself "by an indissoluble bond." So the members of Christ "engrafted to their head . . . are never cut off from salvation."[18] Election cannot be properly conceived in separation from Christ.

Hieronymous Zanchius (1516–90)

Zanchius, a native of Italy, wrote at some length of election in Christ in his massive treatise, *De natura Dei*. Discussing Ephesians 1:4 in particular, he considers that the Father did not elect as the Father but as God, since election is a work common to the whole Trinity (*quandoquidem eligere opus est totius Trinitatis commune*). The Son was also included, since there can be no difference here between the Father and Christ because they are both the same God. As for our being chosen "in him," Zanchius says it is clear that we were chosen in Christ, considered neither as God nor as man but as the God-man (*theanthrōpos*). Christ is presented here not as God, since as God he chose us himself (John 13:18). Nor is he considered purely as man. What Paul means is that in election there was a conjunction between the elect and the One who elected, man with God. The Redeemer needed to be God and man simultaneously in his office as Mediator.[19] The Son was predestined and appointed to this office, the decree encompassing his taking human nature into union in the incarnation. So Christ, according to his human nature, was chosen to this great honor, that on account of the union with the Logos he was to be born the Son of God, the Mediator and Savior of the elect.[20] Finally, in this Christ, the Son of God, all the elect

---

16. Ibid., 3.22.7.
17. Ibid., 3.24.5.
18. Ibid., 3.21.7.
19. "Itaque cum sit Apostolus, nos electos fuisse in Christo: Christus proponitur considerandus, non ut purus Deus, neque ut simplex homo: sed ut Deus & homo simul, cum officio Mediatoris aeterno. Proinde non dicit, nos esse electos *en tō logō*, neque in filio hominis: sed *in Christo*. Hoc enim nomen & duas naturas simul, & officium complectitur." Hieronymous Zanchius, *Operum Theologicorum Omnium* (Amsterdam: Stephanus Gamonentus, 1613), 2:535.
20. Ibid., 2:536.

were foreknown, loved, chosen, and predestined to be given the Spirit of adoption and regenerated in the Son.[21]

We note, Zanchius continues, that three particles are used of Christ in this connection: *in him, through him, on account of him* (*en hō, di' hou, di' hon*). Sometimes these are used interchangeably. The first of these signifies Christ as head of the church in whom all the blessings of God the Father repose; all these treasures are communicated to us from eternity. God loves us *in Christ as head of the church*, and owns us as his sons (*pro filiis agnovit*). In this sense we are as Christ is (*nempe per inde atque si reipsa talis essemus, qualis Christus est, iustissimi, sanctissimi, mundissimi, beatissimi*). Such we are in the sight of God (*Tales nos quoque sumus in conspectu Dei, quotquot ille intuetur in Christo, qualis est & ipse Christus*). On the other hand, the second phrase, *through him/whom*, refers to his office of Mediator—for through Christ we are reconciled to God.[22] In short, God did not choose us because Christ died for us, but Christ died for us because God chose us in him.[23] Therefore, we are not elect on account of Christ's merits, since election has priority over what he did and so included his merit in its purview.[24]

Zanchius expresses the same ideas in his commentary on Ephesians, published posthumously in 1595. There he states again that God elected us, and did so in Christ as our head and Mediator. Christ was chosen first as our head; then we were chosen in him. We are not blessed unless it is in Christ our head.[25]

In *De natura Dei*, Zanchius relates the intent of the atonement to election in Christ. For those for whom he died, Christ expiated their sins, and freed them from death. So they receive eternal life through Christ, and are justified and glorified on account of Christ (*propter Christum*). All who were chosen before the foundation of the world were chosen to these things *in Christ*, and so those who were not chosen do not have these benefits.[26] Here

---

21. Ibid.

22. Ibid.

23. "Non enim ideo nos elegit, quia Christus mortuus est pro nobis, sed contra ideo missus est Filius, qui pro nobis moreretur, quia nos elegit in ipso. Unde dicitur Deus sic dilexisse Mundum, ut Filium suum unigenitum dederit ut, quisquis credit in eum, non pereat." Ibid., 2:536–37.

24. Ibid., 2:537.

25. "Sicut igitur non sumus benedicti, nisi in Christo capite: ita etiam non fuimus electi sine Christo, aut ullo ordine naturae extra Christum, sed in Christo, ut in capite . . . Summa haec est: omnem benedictionem nos accepisse in Christo & habere non fuimus electi extra Christum, sed in Christo, ut membra in capite." Ibid., 6:1:11–12.

26. Ibid., 2:498.

Zanchius expresses the point that all the blessings of salvation flow from our being in Christ from before the constitution of the universe, in the eternal electing purpose of the Holy Trinity.

Amandus Polanus (1561–1610)

Synthesizer – his [a person who uses his mind creatively.]

Polanus was a significant theologian of the Reformed church, based at Basel at the end of the sixteenth century and the start of the next. He was no innovator but a synthesizer of Reformed doctrine. As such, he provides a litmus test of what was being taught ministers in the Reformed churches at that time.[27] His *Syntagma Theologiae Christianae* is a massive example of his work, a systematic compendium of his teaching. In it he considers predestination and election at some length.

According to Polanus, the election of Christ is an aspect of predestination "by which God, from eternity, designated his only-begotten Son to be also Son of God according to his human nature, and head of angels and humans."[28] The whole Trinity made this decree, and so was the efficient cause. The Father elected us, not as the Father but as God, because election is not strictly a work of the person of the Father but of the whole Trinity, of which the Father is the *principium*, the source (*sed ut Deus, quandoquidem electio est totius Sacrosanctiae Trinitatis commune opus, cuius principium est Pater*). The Son (Polanus refers to John 13:18; 15:16, 19) and the Holy Spirit (John 3:6; Acts 13:2; 1 Cor. 6:11; 12:3, 13; Eph. 4:4) also chose us in union with the Father.[29] This election of Christ is entirely gratuitous. It is not for any merit performed by humanity. Its end is the glory of the Father. Christ is contemplated as the Son of God according to both natures. According to his divine nature, he is from the Father by generation (*ex Patri generatione*), so he is not chosen as Son of God according to his divine nature. According to his human nature, however, he is eternally elected, created to the image of God, to the grace of personal union with the eternal Son. This election of

---

27. See Robert Letham, "Amandus Polanus: A Neglected Theologian?" *SCJ* 21 (1990): 463–76; Muller calls him "a theologian of considerable stature" in *Christ and the Decree*, 130, and "the most compendious systematic theologian of the early orthodox period" of Reformed scholasticism. Richard A. Muller, *After Calvin: Studies in the Development of a Theological Tradition* (Oxford: Oxford University Press, 2003), 148.

28. ". . . est praedestinatio qua Deus Filium suum unigenitum designavit ab aeterno, ut etiam quo ad suam humanam natura esset Filius Dei & caput Angelorum & hominesque." Amandus Polanus, *Syntagma Theologiae Christianae* (Geneva: Petri Auberti, 1612), 1:678. He cites in support Isaiah 42:1; Matthew 12:18; and 1 Peter 1:20; 2:5.

29. Polanus, *Syntagma*, 1:681.

Christ is the foundation of the election of angels and human beings (*Electio Christi est fundamentum & firmamentum electionis Angelorum & hominum*).[30] It is Christ as our Mediator who is chosen.[31]

The election of humans can be divided into two parts, Polanus thinks.[32] There is the general election of a nation, such as Israel, and there is special election, by which God ordains to eternal life whoever he chooses in his free benevolence.[33] In support, he cites Athanasius, in his *Orationes contra Arianos*, 3:1, in his statement that our life is founded in no other way than in Christ before the ages existed, for it is through Christ that the ages were created.[34] He insists not merely that Christ is chosen as the means by which we were to be saved but that the election took place *in him* (*Nec enim Paulus dicit, elegit nos per ispum, sed elegit nos in ipso*).[35]

Polanus answers the charges of Jacobus Arminius—in an uncanny pre-echo of the attacks of Karl Barth on the Reformed doctrine of election—that this doctrine of election has no regard for Christ. "Certain people accuse us of having an absolute election [*absolutum electionem*] without respect of Christ by which God, without respect to Christ, chooses some to salvation, and that we oppose election as founded in Christ," he complains (*opponunt electionem in Christo fundatam, fuisque mediis & mediorum taxei ordinatam*). On the contrary, Polanus replies, "we acknowledge with all our heart through the grace of God and openly profess that God chose us in Christ, to be acknowledged through faith, and that our election to salvation was founded in Christ, in whom as our head we are chosen as members of his mystical body."[36]

---

30. Ibid., 1:679.

31. "Electionis subjectum . . . in quo electi sumus, est Christus, non quatenus Deus, nec quatenus nudus homo, sed quatenus *theanthrōpos* & Mediator noster. . . . Ita Christus est vinculum, quo Deus & electi coniunguntur." Ibid., 1:689–90.

32. Polanus was strongly influenced by the philosophical methodology of Petrus Ramus (1514–72), in which knowledge was divisible into component parts, usually dichotomous, so as to be mapped out for ready comprehension. See Letham, "Polanus"; Walter J. Ong, *Ramus, Method and the Decay of Dialogue* (Cambridge, MA: Harvard University Press, 1958); Donald K. McKim, *Ramism in William Perkins' Theology* (New York: Peter Lang, 1987).

33. Polanus, *Syntagma*, 1:680.

34. "Athanasium sensisse nos esse in Christo electos, quia Christus est fundamentum in quo electio & tota instauratio nostri fundata est." Ibid., 1:686. One might add Athanasius, *Orations against the Arians*, 2:70.

35. Polanus, *Syntagma*, 1:686.

36. "Atqui nos agnoscimus toto corde per Dei gratiam & aperte profitemur, quod Deus nos elegerit in Christo per fidem agnoscendo ac quod electio nostra ad salutem aeternam fundata sit in Christo, in quo tanquam in capite nos tanquam membra mysticii corporis eius gratiose electi sumus." Ibid., 1:690.

Polanus agrees with Zanchius that election consists, first, in the choosing by the entire Trinity of Christ as Mediator and Savior. This includes the assumption by the Son of human nature in the incarnation, and his entire work for us and our salvation. All of it is embraced by the term *in Christ*. Then, second, God chooses to save those upon whom he sets his free and sovereign love and does so in union with Christ their head and Mediator. At no time are they contemplated in any other state than in him.

Thomas Goodwin (1600–1680)

Goodwin, a prominent member of the Westminster Assembly and an independent in his ecclesiology, wrote in his commentary on Ephesians in similar vein to Zanchius and Polanus. In election Christ was a common person, as the head of the elect. He was chosen first, and at the same time we in him, before the foundation of the world. As a common person, he was the Son of God who was to become incarnate; by the decree of God he was "pitched upon and singled out to assume our nature, and to sustain the person of a Head before God in the meanwhile."[37] God, in the act of choosing, gave us to Christ, and in giving us to Christ he chose us. "In a word, as in the womb head and members are not conceived apart, but together, as having relation each to the other, so were we and Christ, as making up one mystical body unto God, formed together in that eternal womb of election. So that God's choice did completely terminate itself on him and us; us with him, and yet us in him." As a result we have a representative existence in Christ from everlasting by virtue of his being considered as a common head.[38]

The Westminster Confession of Faith (1643–47)

The divines clearly express their belief, following Scripture, that election is in Christ, although it is not strongly emphasized. It is seen in their presentation of a marked disparity between election and preterition (passing by). The latter is directly connected with the sin of the nonelect and is in perfect accord with God's justice. Election, on the other hand, is entirely a

---

37. Thomas Goodwin, *An Exposition of Ephesians Chapter 1 to 2:10* (n.p.: Sovereign Grace Book Club, 1958), 69–72.
38. Ibid., 74–75.

matter of free grace and love. The elect are chosen in Christ; the nonelect are left to their own sins. Election is "all to the praise of his glorious grace," while preterition is "to the praise of his glorious justice." In the latter, the nonelect receive what is due to them for their own sin. In the former, the elect receive what is due to Christ, in whom they are chosen. Both are in accord with justice; in election the justice is gracious because it is freely given in and through the Mediator (WCF 3.5–7).[39]

Herman Bavinck (1854–1921)

Bavinck, in his *Reformed Dogmatics*, agrees with Zanchius and Polanus that "the church and Christ are jointly chosen, in one and the same decree, in fellowship with and for each other (Eph. 1:4)."[40] Moreover, "the elect are not viewed separately, that is, atomistically, but as a single organism. They constitute the people of God, the body of Christ, the temple of the Holy Spirit. They are, accordingly, elect *in Christ* (Eph. 1:4), to be members of his body. Hence both Christ and the church are included in the decree of predestination."[41] He cites Augustine, in his *On the Predestination of the Saints*, in support. Bavinck is clear that Christ, unlike us, was not the recipient of God's mercy from sin and misery but agrees that it is appropriate to speak of his being elected, since he was ordained to the office of Mediator and to assume into union human nature. Additionally, Bavinck continues, there is the consistent witness of Scripture to our being chosen *in Christ*,[42] and that all other benefits flow from him.[43] Whatever their different nuances, Reformed theologians were agreed that Christ and his church, the mystical Christ, together constitute the real object of election.[44] The inclusion of angels in election, as Polanus did, only serves to indicate their strong conviction that election—and the blessings that follow from it—embraces not only the redemption of man but also the renovation of the cosmos.[45]

---

39. Robert Letham, *The Westminster Assembly: Reading Its Theology in Historical Context* (Phillipsburg, NJ: P&R Publishing, 2009), 186–87.
40. Herman Bavinck, *Reformed Dogmatics*, vol. 2, *God and Creation* (Grand Rapids: Baker Academic, 2004), 401.
41. Ibid., 402–3.
42. Ibid., 403.
43. Ibid., 404.
44. Ibid.
45. Ibid., 404–5.

Union with Christ and Justification

Since election is in union with Christ, it follows that all other aspects of the accomplishment and application of salvation are to be seen in connection with union with Christ as well. We have already caught a glimpse of how this relates to the atonement. Because the atoning death of Christ is in many ways the foundation stone of our justification, we will now consider how the latter is related to union with Christ.

The Relationship between Justification and Faith

Since justification is only by faith, faith is logically prior to justification. Justification is commonly described in Reformed and Lutheran theology as by faith alone. This, as Tony Lane suggests, is better expressed as justification only by faith. The point is that faith is never alone.[46] The Holy Spirit, who gives us the gift of saving faith, always produces fruit in those who receive it. Sanctification, while distinct, is an inseparable concomitant of justification. Justification, however, is only through faith. The exclusive particle, *alone*, is intended to stress that justification is grounded in Christ, in his obedience reckoned or imputed to us, and that it is received through no other means than faith. This excludes anything in us, including the grace of God imparted to us by the Holy Spirit. Justification only by faith affirms this and also precludes the misunderstanding that the faith through which we receive Christ has no consequent effect on us.

Paul makes it clear that justification is only through faith because it is only by Christ and his obedience; this is so particularly in the early chapters of Romans and in Galatians. He is concerned in the latter letter to combat any idea that we contribute anything to securing our status before God. If anyone were to teach such a thing, he says, let them be accursed (Gal. 1:8–9).

In turn, saving faith is a gift of God, as Paul stresses in Ephesians 2:8–9. Jesus teaches this, too, in John 6:44–45 and 64–65; his conversation with Nicodemus underlines the point that it is the Holy Spirit who grants faith, who brings about birth from above (John 3:1–15). From this, it follows that regeneration, the new birth that the Holy Spirit gives in raising us from death in sin (Eph. 2:1), is prior to faith. In turn, since faith is prior to justification, regeneration has priority to both, justification included. We are left with an

---

46. Anthony N. S. Lane, *Justification by Faith in Catholic-Protestant Dialogue: An Evangelical Assessment* (London: T&T Clark, 2002), 27.

order: regeneration—faith—justification. Does that mean, however, that justification is received through God's work of grace begun *in* us in regeneration? If regeneration has priority to justification, does it not follow that the latter must contemplate the inward work of the Holy Spirit? That is the doctrine taught by the Roman Catholic Church, whereby we are justified on the basis of faith working through love, in terms of the righteousness of Christ *imparted* to us by the Holy Spirit. Protestantism, both Lutheran and Reformed, resisted this idea strenuously. Why was this so?

There were strong theological and biblical reasons for avoiding the impasse created by a strictly logical order such as outlined above. Martin Luther, John Calvin, and Lutherans and Reformed as a whole all stressed that the work of God's grace in us does *not* have regard to justification. Why is this? The answer is that justification *is grounded on Christ*, on his obedience and righteousness. This is outside ourselves and independent of our own personal accomplishment. It is *received* by faith, since in faith we abandon self-reliance and trust in Christ alone for salvation. Because we were by nature dead in sin and under the wrath of God, nothing in us enables us to attain a right status with him, not even if due to his grace. Certainly, God imparts his grace to us by the Holy Spirit's transforming us into his image in Christ. But this has nothing whatever to do with our attaining a right *status* with God. Our justification comes exclusively as a result of the work of Christ, through his obedient life and atoning sufferings and death, sealed and vindicated in his resurrection and ascension. Only faith, looking entirely outside ourselves, is *appropriate* for receiving the gratuitous gift of justification.[47]

The Westminster Confession of Faith on Justification Only by Faith

First, the Confession's chapter 11 begins by relating justification to effectual calling. The latter is the result of the work of God's grace to his elect by which he powerfully and graciously draws them to Christ by the

---

47. We are not talking here about what Calvin describes as God's justification of our good works, those works of obedience that are the result of the gracious work of the Holy Spirit within us and are nevertheless in some way soiled by our own continued sinfulness. This relates more to sanctification; these works can in no way secure for us a right status with God, for they are rather evidences of the grace of God, pardoned and accepted by God in virtue of our union with Christ. See *Institutes*, 3.17.5–10; Lane, *Justification*, 33–36; William B. Evans, *Imputation and Impartation: Union with Christ in American Reformed Theology* (Eugene, OR: Wipf & Stock, 2008), 30–32; Mark A. Garcia, *Life in Christ: Union with Christ and Twofold Grace in Calvin's Theology* (Milton Keynes, UK: Paternoster, 2008), 74–78. Nor are we excluding the point that Calvin makes in *Institutes*, 3.11.10, that it is in union with Christ by faith that we are justified.

Holy Spirit. Thus, justification is freely given, a work of his grace. Here, in WCF 11.1, is a refutation of both the Roman Catholic and Arminian doctrines. Justification does not involve the infusion of righteousness. Instead, it consists in the remission of sins and the accounting righteous of the persons justified. This occurs by imputing to them the obedience and satisfaction of Christ. Thus, justification is forensic, by the imputation or accounting of Christ's righteousness, not renovative by the impartation or infusion of grace, as Rome taught. On the other hand, contrary to Arminian teaching, faith itself is not imputed, nor is any other evangelical obedience involved. This would simply be another form of the Roman Catholic doctrine, for justification would then be related to something present in the one believing, albeit the consequence of grace. This the Confession strenuously opposes, since it does not depend on "any thing wrought in them, or done by them." Justification is based on Christ alone. For their part, the justified simply receive and rest on Christ and his righteousness by faith. This faith itself is the gift of God. Faith is appropriate to justification, since it is described in WCF 14.2 as "accepting, receiving, and resting upon Christ alone for justification, sanctification, and eternal life, by virtue of the covenant of grace." Faith looks to Christ alone; it does not contemplate the works of grace or the self. It answers from the human side the exclusively gracious, objective, and forensic nature of justification in Christ and his righteousness alone.

In WCF 11.2, faith, receiving and resting on Christ alone for salvation, is the only instrument of justification. This is in alignment with the insistence in WCF 11.1 that justification is grounded only in Christ, not in anything present in the justified, not even if it be by grace in evangelical obedience. Faith is the only instrument of justification because Christ is its only ground. As the later popular hymn "My Hope Is Built on Nothing Less" had it, "On Christ, the solid rock, I stand; all other ground is sinking sand."

In order to balance the equation, the section adds that saving faith is never alone in the one who is justified but is always accompanied by other saving graces. It works through love. It is living faith, for without works faith is dead. In short, the believer is a repentant believer or he is no believer at all. The question then arises as to what effect these other graces have in relation to justification. If the faith through which we are justified is always accompanied by love, does not love justify? If the one with saving faith is also repentant, should not repentance have something to do with justification? The Confession has already given us the answer: these things have nothing to do with justification. They are inseparable from the faith that justifies but are disconnected from the justification received through faith. They define the person justified, not the justification of the person. They describe the one who has faith, but do not constitute his standing before God received through faith.[48]

The divines emphasize the sheer grace of God in justification in WCF 11.3. Christ made full and complete satisfaction to the Father's justice for all the justified. This secures their complete acquittal and the perfection of their righteousness, which is Christ's righteousness reckoned to them. This is entirely of God's free grace. The exact justice and rich grace of God meet together.

Nor is faith itself imputed for justification, as Arminians held. If that were true, faith would be a work and the gratuitous nature of justification jeopardized. Instead, faith is merely an instrument by which Christ and his righteousness is received. Faith is the appropriate means of reception, since it simply receives and rests on Christ alone (WCF 14.1–2). Once again, we see how union with Christ fits perfectly with justification only by faith. Precisely because the righteous status is achieved only by Christ and is reckoned or imputed by God to his elect, who have done nothing to merit it, it is only by faith—abandoning self and trusting only to Christ—that this becomes actual to the elect.

The Westminster Larger Catechism

Thomas F. Torrance accuses the Assembly of departing from Calvin's teaching and that of the Scots Reformation, in which justification is held inseparably with union with Christ. He fails to consider WLC 65–90.[49] It is astonishing that a scholar so careful and meticulous throughout his vast corpus should be so neglectful on a matter such as this much closer to home.

The Catechism considers the whole of the application of salvation to us by the Holy Spirit—the *ordo salutis,* as it is called—to be an aspect of union with Christ. Whereas in the Confession justification is the first of the blessings of salvation, followed by adoption, sanctification, perseverance, and assurance, the Catechism treats them all as aspects of our union and communion with Christ

---

48. Latter-day exponents of this passage, who argue that evangelical graces should be considered in relation to justification, have wrenched the words from their immediate polemical context and thus distorted the Assembly's teaching, which in this case was accepted right across the board. See Letham, *Westminster Assembly*, 250–76.

49. Thomas F. Torrance, *Scottish Theology: From John Knox to John McLeod Campbell* (Edinburgh: T&T Clark, 1996), 144.

in grace and glory (65–90). Obviously, the members of the Assembly saw no discrepancy in these two perspectives. They understood them as complementary, not competitive. The divines were hardly schizophrenic in their theology.

Edward Morris makes the point very clearly that union with Christ undergirds justification by faith. He points out that pardon itself is not enough for salvation—for there is still the sinner who remains corrupt. Hence, "nothing but his union with Christ through faith can render him worthy of such cordial acceptance before the throne of the Father." So God by his Spirit does not infuse righteousness into regenerate souls so as to make them instantly holy; he does not treat them as holy by imputing faith to them, or evangelical obedience in any form; but he accounts and treats them as holy by virtue of their union with Christ established through faith. In support he cites the Augsburg Confession, the Formula of Concord, the Second Helvetic Confession, the Scots Confession, the Thirty-nine Articles, and the Irish Articles.[50]

The divines are treading here the path previously trodden by Calvin. We cited him as advocating the imputation of the righteousness of Christ in justification. In his *Institutes* he does so again in direct connection with union with Christ. In refuting the extreme Lutheran Osiander, he says:

> Therefore, that joining together of Head and members, that indwelling of Christ in our hearts—in short, that mystical union—are accorded by us the highest degree of importance, so that Christ, having been made ours, makes us sharers with him in the gifts with which he has been endowed. We do not, therefore, contemplate him outside ourselves from afar in order that his righteousness may be imputed to us but because we put on Christ and are engrafted into his body—in short, because he deigns to make us one with him. For this reason, we glory that we have fellowship of righteousness with him.[51]

From another angle, in his commentary on 1 Corinthians 1:30 Calvin remarks that justification and sanctification are distinguishable, but yet "those gifts of grace go together as if tied by an inseparable bond, so that if anyone tries to separate them, he is, in a sense, tearing Christ to pieces." Tony Lane has compared

---

50. Edward D. Morris, *Theology of the Westminster Symbols: A Commentary Historical, Doctrinal, Practical on the Confession of Faith and Catechisms, and the Related Formularies of Presbyterian Churches* (Columbus, OH, 1900), 442–43.

51. *Institutes*, 3.11.10. For an extensive study on Calvin's teaching on union with Christ, see Garcia, *Life in Christ*.

them to two legs of a pair of trousers.[52] Paul, Calvin states, ascribes to Christ alone the fulfilment of all—righteousness, holiness, wisdom, and redemption.

WLC 70, like the Confession, describes justification as an act of God's free grace to sinners. In this it is an aspect of union with Christ in grace. In union with Christ our sins are pardoned and our persons accepted as righteous. This is only due to the perfect obedience and full satisfaction of Christ imputed, received by faith alone. The nuance the Catechism brings is that it is received in union with Christ. In the background is Christ as "a publick person" who represents his people. His perfect obedience was exercised on their behalf, his sufferings on behalf of the elect. It would be tempting to see here also some of the dynamic aspects of union with Christ that are present in the NT, but as far as I can see there is no specific evidence that this was discussed. Indeed, the care with which the debates on the Articles sought to safeguard justification from the Roman Catholic position, together with the denial of any instrumental role for imparted grace, leads in the opposite direction.

So much is borne out by Q. 71. Here justification is said to be of free grace, although Christ made full satisfaction to God's justice. This is so, first, since God accepts the fulfillment of his law from a surety; second, because he himself provided the surety; this surety was, third, his own Son; fourth, he requires nothing from them for justification but faith; this in turn, fifth, is his gift. The Catechism brings together law and grace, and shows clearly how the full provisions of the law are fulfilled in a way by which God's grace is clearly dominant. Man had sinned, breaking God's law and incurring guilt and condemnation. Christ the Son, in mercy, stepped in, took the place of his elect, fulfilled the law, bore its penalty on their behalf. Thus the claims of God's justice were completely discharged, and in this way his people are delivered from their dire natural condition and given a new status, invested with the righteousness of Christ. Moreover, all this is grounded on Christ's being fully man, one with us through his incarnation, and thus our head and representative. Furthermore, not only was all that he did done for us, but because of our union with him, we are in him in all that he did. Union with Christ is no more incompatible with forensic justification than justification is incompatible with sanctification. This undermines Torrance's caricature of Westminster as conveying a harsh legal view of God and salvation, which he could do only by ignoring the WLC.

For the rationale for this we could cite the passages already mentioned, such as Ephesians 1:3–14, where Paul unfolds the entirety of salvation as

52. Lane, *Justification*, 18.

received in Christ. More specifically, at the climax of his discussion of justification in Romans 4, he states that Christ was "delivered up for our offenses and raised for our justification" (v. 25). As Christ on the cross died to sin (Rom. 6:1f.)—in our place, on our behalf, and as one with us—so his resurrection, his public vindication by the Father, was in our place, on our behalf, and as one with us. Consequently, we died to sin in the death of Christ and rose to newness of life in his resurrection.

Classic Reformed Theology

We have already seen how Zanchius presents the point that Christ was chosen and predestined to be head of the elect. This means, Zanchius continues, that all spiritual blessings, such as Paul intends in his comprehensive statement in Ephesians 1:3, are received by us precisely and exclusively in union with Christ our head. This includes justification:

> Christ, as man and mediator, was before all of us chosen and predestined to be the head of all the predestined, that is, the whole church. Consequently, it means that now through Christ and on account of Christ the Mediator we are in reality blessed with all spiritual blessings in the heavenly places, called, justified and glorified: thus also we were from eternity foreknown by the Father, loved, chosen and predestined to calling, justification, and glorification in Christ the mediator as in our head.[53]

Hence, before the foundation of the world we were predestined *to this justification in Christ*: those who now are justified are so through and on account of Christ.[54] Indeed, all the good things we possess, outside of us or in us, are in Christ, and only in Christ.[55]

Amandus Polanus also connects justification with election and affirms that both are equally to be understood as aspects of our union with Christ. In

53. "Christum, qua homo & Mediator est, fuisse ante omnes nos electum & praedestinatum ut caput esset omnium praedestinandorum, hoc est, totius Ecclesiae. Deinde significatur, sicut nunc per & propter Christum Mediatorem, reapse benedicimur omni benedictione spirituali, in colestibus, vocamur, iustificamur & tandem glorificabimur: sic etiam in hoc eodem Christo Mediatore, tanquam in capite nos fuisse ab aeterno a Patre praecognotos, amatos, electos, & ad vocationem, iustificationem, glorificationem, omnesque spirituales benedictiones praedestinatos." Zanchius, *Operum*, 2:537.

54. "Sicut qui nunc iustificantur per & propter Christum, ante Mundi constitutionem fuerunt ad hanc iustificationem in Christo praedestinati: ita qui nunquam per & propter Christum iustificantur, eos fuisse nunquam in Christo ad iustificationem electos." Ibid.

55. "Quicquid igitur bonorum, aut habemus extra nos, aut in nobis possidemus, possessurve fuimus: totum illud nobis fuisse & preparatum & donatum in Christo: extra Christum autem omnino nihil." Ibid.

election God from eternity gave to Christ those to whom he willed to have mercy and to give eternal life. This entailed their adoption as sons in Christ, their justification in Christ, and their glorification.[56] So we are regenerated and justified through the same decree in which we were elected (*per eundem & electi sumus ad vitam aeternam*).[57]

Heinrich Heppe lists a number of representative theologians who also made the same connection.[58] He cites John Henry Heidegger, who wrote in 1696 that those God implanted in Christ are regarded by the Father as though they possessed all that Christ had done and suffered, and that those united to Christ are partakers in the righteousness Christ secured by his blood; and Hendrik van Maastricht, who affirmed in 1714 that those united to Christ are regarded as righteous by God and that for those who are in Christ, Christ is said to have been made righteousness by God. That these statements cannot be taken as implying the Roman Catholic doctrine of justification on the ground of the righteousness of Christ imparted to us is obvious. No such controversy surrounded their views. Rather, the righteousness is alien to us, for as Paul stated, Christ is made to us righteousness from God (1 Cor. 1:30).[59]

Rowland Stedman (1630?–73)

Stedman considered union with Christ to be foundational to all the covenant blessings given in Christ, as WLC 65–90 did.[60] On justification, he affirms that "without union with him, there can be no justification through the blood, nor clothing with his righteousness for acceptance with the Lord."[61] Our righteousness is in Christ; therefore, we must be in him in order to

---

56. "Electio hominum aeternum servandorum, est praedestinatio quae Deus ab aeterno dedit Christo eos homines quorum voluit misereri, et illis daret vitam aeternam. . . . In filios adoptare in Christo, iustificare in Christo & glorificare vellet, ut Christi gloriam in aeternum spectent, & in ipso sint particeps caelestis haereditatis & vitae aeternae." Polanus, *Syntagma*, 1:680.

57. Ibid., 1:681.

58. Heinrich Heppe, *Reformed Dogmatics: Set Out and Illustrated from the Sources*, trans. Ernst Bizer and G. T. Thomson (Grand Rapids: Baker, 1950), 543.

59. See the pertinent discussion in Richard B. Gaffin Jr., *By Faith, Not by Sight: Paul and the Order of Salvation* (Milton Keynes, UK: Paternoster, 2006), 50–52. Gaffin states, "In union with Christ, his righteousness is the ground of my being justified. That is, in my justification his righteousness becomes my righteousness. But this . . . is virtually and necessarily to be at the notion of imputation . . . An imputative aspect is integral, indispensable to the justification given in union with Christ."

60. Rowland Stedman, *The Mystical Union of Believers with Christ, or A Treatise Wherein That Great Mystery and Privilege of the Saints Union with the Son of God Is Opened* (London: W. R. for Thomas Parkhurst, at the Golden-Bible on London-Bridge, under the gate, 1668), 200, Wing / 335:13.

61. Ibid., 202.

partake of his righteousness. He cites Ephesians 1:6–7 to the effect that acceptance and redemption are in Christ.[62] In order to be justified, due to the infinite holiness of God, we must produce a perfect righteousness. "God doth not pronounce men righteous when they are not; but first he maketh them righteous, and then receiveth them as such, and pronounceth them to be such."[63] In other words, Stedman is denying that justification can ever be a legal fiction. But since the fall, it has not been possible for man to be just before God, except with the obedience and sufferings of Jesus Christ, the Mediator.[64] The point is that we cannot be pardoned and accepted by God until that righteousness is ours and is made over to us. This is done by imputation, by which God reckons the righteousness of Christ to his people as if it were their own, and accounts to them Christ's sufferings and satisfaction as if they had suffered and made satisfaction themselves.[65] Moreover, no one "can have the righteousness of Christ imputed to them, *but only such as are in Christ*; such as are united to him, and made one with him; for, Sirs, *Union is the very ground of imputation*."[66] Stedman points to the relationship between Adam and the race. Adam's sin would not have been laid to our account unless we had been legally and by imputation in Adam, "so we cannot have the obedience of Christ made over to us and reputed as ours; but first in order of nature we must be in him."[67] Therefore, for Stedman, union with Christ is an indispensable necessity for justification to take place. Furthermore, in no way does it undermine the gratuitous nature of justification, since it is the righteousness of *Christ* that *alone* avails. It is not the *union* with Christ that justifies but the union with *Christ*. The making righteous that Stedman mentions is not due to the imparted grace of the Holy Spirit, but it is *the righteousness of Christ* that, by virtue of union with him, is really, truly, and actually ours.

In Contrast to Rome and Lutheranism

From this it should be clear that union with Christ cannot undermine justification only by faith. The classic Reformed statements bring both

62. Ibid., 202–3.
63. Ibid., 206.
64. Ibid., 207.
65. Ibid., 210–11.
66. Ibid., 213.
67. Ibid.

together. On the one hand, they differ from a purely external justification as is seen in Lutheranism. In this construction, union with Christ is excluded, for it follows justification as its effect. Justification is entirely outside ourselves, a forensic decision affecting the individual. It is the absolute center of the gospel, if not the gospel itself. On the other hand, the Reformed oppose the Roman Catholic doctrine in which we are held to be justified on account of the righteousness of Christ infused into us by the grace of the Holy Spirit. This is a conflation of justification and sanctification and roots justification in something God does *within* us. Hence, for Rome justification is not by faith alone but by faith working through love, works of evangelical obedience contributing to our justification. This was anathema to the Reformed; as I have argued elsewhere, no one at the Westminster Assembly gave this a moment's approval.[68] Union with Christ, as the Reformed understand it, neither entails nor implies that the grace of God within us is the instrumental means of our justification. It is Christ who justifies, not our faith, nor anything in us, even if that is due to the work of the Spirit. It is by our union with Christ that we benefit from his righteousness; and it is exclusively through faith, which looks away from ourselves to Christ, that we receive it.[69]

Recent Proposals

Space prevents me from interacting at length with recent discussions of the relationship between union with Christ and justification. In large measure, this is because the purpose of this book is to present a picture of how I understand union with Christ to relate to the broader theological context. In considering recent discussion on this matter, this purpose would be lost, since there are a number of points of contention in these proposals and one could not, as a result, avoid being preoccupied by different agendas. At a later date we may be able to discuss them.[70]

---

68. Letham, *Westminster Assembly*, 271–72.

69. For an excellent discussion of this question, see Lane G. Tipton, "Union with Christ and Justification," in *Justified in Christ: God's Plan for Us in Justification*, ed. K. Scott Oliphint (Fearn, Ross-shire, UK: Mentor, 2007), 23–50.

70. See, inter alia, Evans, *Imputation and Impartation*; Gaffin, *By Faith, Not by Sight*; Garcia, "Imputation and the Christology of Union with Christ," 219–51; Michael S. Horton, *Covenant and Salvation: Union with Christ* (Louisville: Westminster John Knox Press, 2007); Tipton, "Union with Christ and Justification," 23–50; Bruce L. McCormack, "What's at Stake in the Current Debates over Justification? The Crisis of Protestantism in the West," in *Justification: What's at Stake in the Current Debates*, ed. Mark Husbands and Daniel J. Treier (Downers Grove, IL: InterVarsity Press, 2004), 81–117.

Summary

(1) Union with Christ is based on Christ's being our covenant head and is established by his sharing our nature.

(2) Since he is our head and representative, who shares our humanity, all that he did in his earthly ministry was done as a substitute and representative.

(3) Yet our union with Christ goes much further than this. Since he shares our nature, and since the Holy Spirit unites us to him, all that he did and does is in union with us. He took our place under the wrath of God, while we take his place as sons of the Father. He is the captain of the team of which we are members. When the captain scores the winning goal in the final minute of stoppage time, the whole team participates in the captain's actions.

(4) This union is the ground of our whole salvation, justification included. We receive a right status before God, since we are incorporated into the Son of God himself. All that he did is ours.

We were and are considered by God to be in Christ at the point he acted.

Union with Christ and Transformation

Not only does our union with Christ have external aspects, but it also transforms us from within. When Christ died and rose from the dead, we died and rose with him, and so our status and existence was dramatically changed. Since, following Christ's ascension, the Holy Spirit was sent to bring us to spiritual life and indwell and renew us, our participation in Christ's death and resurrection is vitally dynamic and transformative. These two elements are inseparable.[1] This follows from who Christ is and what he has done. He, the Son of God incarnate, alive from the dead as our Mediator and Savior, was publicly vindicated by the Father in his resurrection. We share, by grace, his status as the Son who achieved our salvation. With that status comes his risen and indestructible life, which is made ours by the Holy Spirit.[2]

Biblical Texts

We saw, in Ephesians 1:3–14, how Paul explains that our whole salvation is to be understood as in union with Christ. He does not stop there. In Ephesians 1:15f., he prays that the power of God seen in Christ's resurrection would be at work in the life experience of those united to him. God raised

---

1. As Lane Tipton puts it, "Union with Christ allows Paul to speak in relational and judicial categories simultaneously, without conflating either into the other." Lane G. Tipton, "Union with Christ and Justification," in *Justified in Christ: God's Plan for Us in Justification*, ed. K. Scott Oliphint (Fearn, Ross-shire, UK: Mentor, 2007), 38.

2. This principle is well expressed by Michael Horton, who considers Christ's resurrection as a forensic verdict by the Father. Michael S. Horton, *Covenant and Salvation: Union with Christ* (Louisville: Westminster John Knox Press, 2007), 267–307.

Jesus from the dead, something that only he could do. It was tantamount to a new creation. Moreover, he raised him to the place of highest authority, far above all the angelic powers, far above the entire creation, so that he might be all in all. Paul asks the Father that this same power would be displayed in the Ephesian believers, that they would experience the same power that raised Christ from the dead and exalted him as Lord. Their union with Christ is a real and dynamic experience. Elsewhere Paul describes the resurrection of Christ as effected by the Father through the Holy Spirit (Rom. 8:10–11). This experience of resurrection from death in sin to sitting with Christ in the heavenly places (Eph. 2:1–7) flows from the same engagement of all three persons of the Trinity as when Christ was raised at the first Easter. The Father raises us in union with Christ the Son, effected by the Holy Spirit.

Paul also refers to the ongoing process that follows. In 2 Corinthians 3:18, he writes that we are being transformed *into* the image of God. Christ himself *is* the image of God (2 Cor. 4:4; cf. Col. 1:15). We are being changed to be like the glorified Christ, the second Adam. This happens gradually and progressively, "from one degree of glory to another." Glory is that which belongs exclusively to God; it is closely connected with the image of God. It happens as we behold "as in a mirror the glory of the Lord." The context refers this to the risen Christ. The One who changes us, transforming us into the image of the glorified Christ, is "the Lord, the Spirit," who in the previous sentence is inseparably identified with the risen Christ (vv. 17–18). Indeed, Jesus had taught that the principal ministry of the Holy Spirit is to testify of him. Once again, we see the whole Trinity engaged to make us like Christ. Union with Christ is not only extrinsic, for it has deeply personal effects. We are not only united with Christ in the sense that what he has done we have done because of our being one with him. Being united to Christ, we are also in the process of being made to be like him. When he returns, "we shall be like him, for we shall see him as he is" (1 John 3:2).

Union with Christ in his death and resurrection also has a present impact on the life experience of Paul in his apostolic ministry. He experiences the death of Christ in his body as he suffers in union with him. The persecutions, the rejection, the imminence of death on so many occasions display his sharing the sufferings of Christ on behalf of the church (2 Cor. 1:8–11; Phil. 1:12–26; Col. 1:24f.). At the same time, he also experiences the life of Christ and the power of his resurrection in the midst of these sufferings (2 Cor. 4:7–18). Nor does he limit this to his own account, despite his unique role as an apostle. On the contrary, this is something in common with regular Christian experience. He presents these things in an inclusive sense, in the first-person plural, setting before his readers his own experience as a model and an encouragement to others in their own struggles. While he focuses on public ministry, it is, by extension, relevant to all who are united to Christ by the Holy Spirit through faith. We will return to this theme in chapter 6.

Sanctification in Its Primary Sense as Spatial

At root, sanctification is a spatial concept. It entails being purchased by Christ and so being the property of God. We have been transferred from the domain of darkness to the kingdom of God's beloved Son (Col. 1:13). We have been redeemed—bought with a price—and so we are not our own (1 Cor. 6:19–20). Therefore, we have been separated from sin and the world and belong specifically and particularly to God (Rom. 6:1–23). We belong to God in Christ—all that he did and does is for us, and we are with him and in him. In this sense, sanctification is definitive; it has already taken place in Christ by the power of the Holy Spirit. Because Christ died, we have died to sin in union with him. Since he rose from the dead, we have risen to newness of life in him.[3] By the power of the Holy Spirit, this is a dynamic reality as well as an objective fact.

Sanctification in Its Ethical Sense

Sanctification also has an ongoing element. This is its most commonly recognized aspect. It is most evident in ethical terms. The letters of Paul are replete with injunctions about how we are to live. The possibility that we can do this, at least in part, is due to the Holy Spirit's work within us, transforming us into the image of God (Eph. 4:24; Col. 3:10). The ethical characteristics Paul enjoins he also describes as "the fruit of the Spirit" (Gal. 5:22f.). Here again, the dynamic of union with Christ comes to present expression in the life experience of believers. Christ has risen, never again to submit to death. So we, in union with him, are no longer subject to the domain of sin and death,

---

3. See John Murray, "Definitive Sanctification," *CTJ* 2, 1 (1967): 5–21. This was republished in John Murray, *Collected Writings of John Murray*, vol. 2, *Select Lectures in Systematic Theology* (Edinburgh: Banner of Truth, 1977), 277–84. Note the strong criticisms of Murray's innovative concept of definitive sanctification by J. V. Fesko, "Sanctification and Union with Christ: A Reformed Perspective," *EQ* 82, 3 (2010): 197–214.

and so grow "more and more" (as WCF 13.1 puts it) in conformity to Christ by the inward work of the Spirit through the means of grace that God has provided: the ministry of the Word, the sacraments, and prayer (WSC 88).

Union with Christ and the *Ordo Salutis*

In recent years, there has been much discussion of how union with Christ relates to the *ordo salutis* ("order of salvation") adopted by Reformed theology since the seventeenth century, a tool for understanding analytically the way in which we become Christians and remain in the faith. The various elements have been related to each other in a logical manner, reflecting what are perceived as the biblical parameters that govern them.

Usually, effectual calling and regeneration are placed first. Calling is the powerful action of the Father drawing us from death to life in Christ. Typically, it embraces the whole process of what in popular terms is called *conversion*, whatever form that may take. Regeneration is the hidden action of the Holy Spirit in bringing us from death in sins to life, making us a new creation (2 Cor. 5:17). There are various explanations of how these two elements are related: some consider that calling has priority; others think regeneration comes first.[4] A slight complication is that John Calvin terms the whole reception of salvation on our side as regeneration.

Faith, justification, and adoption are all seen as happening at the start of the Christian life. Faith, as a gift of God, is a consequence of regeneration. This is counter to Arminianism and all forms of semi-Pelagianism, which hold that fallen man retains the ability to believe the gospel with assistance from divine grace after he has taken the first step. In contrast, Reformed theology maintains that fallen man is dead in trespasses and sins and so has no ability of himself to bring himself to spiritual life. It requires a work of God to raise the dead, and this is done by the Spirit in regeneration. The newly regenerate person will then respond in faith to the gospel and be justified on the basis of the work of Jesus Christ. Simultaneously with justification, he or she will become a child of God, adopted into his family and so enabled to call God "Father" (Rom. 8:15–16; Gal. 4:6). Justification is legal and juridical; adoption is legal, too, but with a permanent filial outcome.

---

4. R. W. A. Letham, "Calling," in *New Dictionary of Theology*, ed. Sinclair B. Ferguson, David F. Wright, and J. I. Packer (Leicester, UK: Inter-Varsity Press, 1988), 119–20.

Sanctification follows, lifelong, buttressed by perseverance. We are "kept by the power of God through faith" (1 Peter 1:5). There is responsibility on our part, to persevere in faith. The power for this comes from God. So we grow in the grace and knowledge of Jesus Christ throughout the course of our lives, through temptations, sufferings, and all kinds of trials. Hence, the term *perseverance of the saints* is appropriate; it is those who are sanctified who persist, come what may. Finally, glorification occurs at the resurrection and the return of Christ, when we are finally brought to the destiny that God has planned for us from eternity, transformed into the image of God in Christ.

This *ordo salutis*—effectual calling, regeneration, faith, justification, adoption, sanctification, glorification—or some such arrangement comes to expression in a document such as the WCF, from chapters 10–18. The problem is that union with Christ does not seem to fit into it very easily. Indeed, John Murray, in his book *Redemption Accomplished and Applied*, included a chapter at the very end where he indicated that it was difficult to decide how to handle the matter.[5] In fairness to the Westminster Assembly, it considered the entire *ordo salutis* to come under the umbrella of union and communion with Christ in grace and glory (WLC 65–90). In so doing, it recognized that union with Christ is not one aspect of the process of salvation but is the overall context in which all aspects are to be seen.

Influenced by the biblical theology of Geerhardus Vos, Richard B. Gaffin Jr. has raised questions about the *ordo salutis*. He has cautiously suggested the possibility that it needed recasting. This is in view of Paul's insistence that the center of the biblical revelation of salvation is the death and resurrection of Christ. Our union with him in those epochal events, viewed in the eschatological sense that Paul gives them, should shape our soteriology, Gaffin suggests.[6] Gaffin has not intended to undermine the doctrine of justification only by faith, but rather to see the order of salvation in a manner compatible with the Pauline view of redemptive history. Others, influenced by Gaffin, have voiced similar proposals.[7]

---

5. John Murray, *Redemption Accomplished and Applied* (London: Banner of Truth, 1961), 161–62.

6. Richard B. Gaffin Jr., *The Centrality of the Resurrection: A Study in Paul's Soteriology* (Grand Rapids: Baker, 1978), 135–43; Richard B. Gaffin Jr., *By Faith, Not by Sight: Paul and the Order of Salvation* (Milton Keynes, UK: Paternoster, 2006).

7. William B. Evans, *Imputation and Impartation: Union with Christ in American Reformed Theology* (Eugene, OR: Wipf & Stock, 2008); Tim J. Trumper, "Covenant Theology and Constructive Calvinism," *WTJ* 64 (2002): 387–404.

While Gaffin's concerns are important ones—and this book, from a different perspective, stresses the centrality of union with Christ—it would be a mistake to abandon the concept of the *ordo salutis*. Certainly, Gaffin does not advocate this. That each element of salvation is received in Christ does not negate a relationship between these constituent elements. Even if all these facets are received, in principle, simultaneously in a single act, there are still connections and relative priorities that they sustain to each other. There are elements at the start of the Christian life (regeneration, saving faith, justification, adoption, sanctification in its definitive sense), allowing for the fact that each has continuing significance and reality. Some aspects of salvation exist mainly in an ongoing way (perseverance, sanctification in its progressive sense, adoption or, better, the sonship that results from adoption). Other elements come into play only at the return of Christ (the resurrection of the body, glorification), while the rest are completed or fulfilled at that point. Yet even here the ultimately final and eschatological aspects of salvation have a present reality, even as those that are largely associated with the commencement of Christian experience are fulfilled only at the end. Thus Paul writes of our having been glorified, using the aorist tense in Romans 8:30. The hymn writer Isaac Watts expressed it well when he wrote in "Come, We That Love the Lord": "The men of grace have found glory begun below; celestial fruits on earthly ground from faith and love doth flow."

The Holy Spirit has been given as an earnest of the final redemption (2 Cor. 1:21–22; Eph. 1:13–14).[8] We have reflected this interrelationship by discussing union with Christ in regeneration, faith, and justification in chapter 4 before considering union with Christ in sanctification, adoption, and glorification here. We will conclude by examining union with Christ in our death and resurrection in the chapter that follows. The fact that union with Christ is paramount, far from requiring that we dispense with the *ordo salutis*, preserves and enhances it by pointing to its integrating feature. The divines at Westminster knew this in the seventeenth century when they combined a logical or orderly *ordo salutis* in WCF 9–18 with the same topics considered as aspects of union and communion with Christ in grace and glory in WLC 65–90.[9] Moreover, it

---

8. Vos writes of the Spirit's proper sphere as "the future aeon; from thence, he projects himself into the present, and becomes a prophecy of himself in his eschatological operations" and as "the element, as it were, in which, as in its circumambient atmosphere the life of the coming aeon shall be lived." Geerhardus Vos, *The Pauline Eschatology* (Grand Rapids: Eerdmans, 1972), 165, 163.

9. See Robert Letham, *The Westminster Assembly: Reading Its Theology in Historical Context* (Phillipsburg, NJ: P&R Publishing, 2009), 242–92.

is at least open to question whether we are simply to follow precisely the same pattern as Paul did. He was not the only biblical author.

Union with Christ and *Theōsis*

Here it may be helpful to reflect on the different ways in which union with Christ from regeneration to glorification has been understood in the Eastern and Western churches. As in some plant forms, cross-fertilization— in this case, of ideas—can be a way to growth and advancement. Recent years have seen an increased interest in the theology of the Eastern church. This has been due to the growing exposure of Orthodoxy in the Western world and to a stream of conversions from Protestantism, largely of those disenchanted by the triviality of much evangelicalism.[10] Central to the Orthodox view of salvation is the doctrine of *theōsis*.[11] Whereas Protestantism in general and the Reformed churches in particular have focused on matters such as the atonement and justification, couched largely in forensic terms and centered on the beginning of Christian experience, the Eastern preoccupation from its earliest days has been on the ongoing and eschatological transformation of the Christian by the Holy Spirit. In the second century, Irenaeus pointed the way, while Athanasius followed him with his celebrated statement concerning the incarnation of Christ: "He became man that we might become God."[12]

An idea such as this sounds alarming to Western Protestant ears. But it has usually been misunderstood. Reformed commentators have frequently considered *theōsis* to entail the pagan notion of *apotheōsis*, humanity being elevated to divine status, undergoing ontological change. Such an idea would carry with it an inevitable blurring of the Creator-creature distinction, foundational to the whole of biblical revelation. In other words, it has been seen by Protestants as man's becoming God in the sense of being changed into the essence of God; this would be a contradiction of the Christian faith. It would negate the classic teaching of the church on the person of Christ, regarding which Eutyches was rejected as a heretic because his claims submerged the humanity of Christ.

10. See Robert Letham, *Through Western Eyes: Eastern Orthodoxy; A Reformed Perspective* (Fearn, Ross-shire, UK: Mentor, 2007).
11. This is often called *deification*.
12. Athanasius, *On the Incarnation*, 54; *PG*, 25:192.

These perceptions of the Eastern teaching on *theōsis* are misleading. Sometimes, it is true, there are grounds for Reformed misgivings. More typically, especially in the Alexandrian teaching of Athanasius and Cyril, *theōsis* encompasses under one umbrella what in Reformed theology is understood to occur in the entire movement of God's grace in transforming us into his image in Christ: regeneration, sanctification, and glorification combined. In Eastern Christianity, this is seen as one seamless process.

The Doctrine of *Theōsis* in Athanasius and Cyril of Alexandria

There were two main strands on this matter in Eastern Christian thought. The first of these, exemplified in Origen and Gregory of Nyssa, moves closer to the idea of *apotheōsis*. In this line of thought, there is a generic human nature that was created by God and is now divinized. Salvation entails being absorbed into God, individuals losing their identity as they are merged into this deified humanity.[13] But another approach was adopted at Alexandria by Athanasius and Cyril. With these two, humans remain humans while deified. They are not merged into God in such a way as to lose their humanity; *theōsis* does not mean becoming God in terms of being. Nor, on the other hand, is it simply communion with God's attributes (or *energies*, in the terms of Gregory Palamas), for this would leave us with an impersonal view of salvation. It is, rather, union and communion with the *persons* of the Trinity. This is achieved in our sharing by grace the relation to the Father that the Son has by nature, thus retaining both personal and human identity.[14] It is with this second line of thought that we will interact, since it provides some insights and produces clarifications that may be helpful for our understanding of what union with Christ does and does not entail.

First, we need to ask what Athanasius actually meant when he wrote that sentence, "He [Christ] became man that we might become God [*autos huiopoiēsen, hina hēmeis theōpoiēthōmen*]." Norman Russell writes that when Athanasius makes comments such as this, "it is either to emphasize the glorious destiny originally intended for the human race, or to explain that the biblical references to 'gods' do not encroach upon the uniqueness of the

---

13. Donald Fairbairn, "Patristic Soteriology: Three Trajectories," *JETS* 50, 2 (June 2007): 297–304.
14. Ibid., 298–310.

Word made flesh."[15] This follows from the uniqueness of the incarnation. The assumption by Christ of human nature into personal union underlies this whole reality. The Son made us sons of the Father and deified man by becoming man himself (*autos huiopoiēsen hēmas tō Patri, kai etheoipoiēse tous anthrōpous genomenos autos anthrōpos*).[16] For Athanasius, by becoming man and receiving a human body, the Son deified that nature in himself. This he did by uniting the nature of man with the nature of God in himself in one person in his incarnation. So first of all is the *theōsis* of the human nature of Christ by the Son in the incarnation. Since from the moment of conception it was taken into personal union by God the Son, the assumed humanity was made capable of union with God. The Logos received a human body so that, Athanasius writes, having renewed it as its Creator, he might deify it in himself and thus bring us all into the kingdom of heaven in his likeness (*hina en heautō theiopoiēsē*). The union was of this kind: he united the nature of the Godhead with the nature of man so that our salvation and deification might be made sure. In other words, Athanasius is arguing that the humanity of Jesus Christ, body and soul, was given the grace of being capable of everlasting personal union with the eternal Son of God.[17] If this were not so, there could have been no incarnation.

This, the *theōsis* of Christ's humanity, is the foundation of our own. It is vital to note here that Athanasius does not mean that Christ's human nature ceased to be human. This could hardly be the case; he says that Christ became man, while he was the staunchest defender of his deity. Athanasius did not intend to say that in becoming man, Christ ceased to be God. Therefore, when he states that we might become God, he cannot mean that we cease to be human, nor that Christ's humanity was not real humanity.

What Athanasius does mean is that all things receive the characteristics of that in which they participate. Hence, by participating in the Holy Spirit, we become holy; by participating in the Logos, we are able to contemplate the Father.[18] This, we may add, follows the principle that a person becomes increasingly like the object that commands his or her worship. Idolaters become like their worthless idols (Ps. 115:4–8; Rom. 1:19–23), so in worshiping the Holy Trinity we become like Christ and eventually will be exactly

15. Norman Russell, *The Doctrine of Deification in the Greek Patristic Tradition* (Oxford: Oxford University Press, 2004), 168.

16. Athanasius, *Orations against the Arians*, 1:38–39; *PG*, 26:92–93.

17. Athanasius, *Against the Arians*, 3:23, 33–34; *PG*, 26:369, 373, 393–97.

18. Athanasius, *Letters to Serapion on the Holy Spirit*, 1:23–24; *PG*, 26:584–89.

like him according to our humanity (2 Cor. 3:18; 1 John 3:1–2). From this, Athanasius continues to maintain that we are participants in Christ and God (*legometha metochoi Christou kai metochoi theou*).[19]

Athanasius's main form of expression is *metochoi* ("partakers"). What does he mean? Russell points out that he normally couples it with an explanatory synonym so as to avoid possible misunderstanding: "Adoption, renewal, salvation, sanctification, grace, transcendence, illumination, and vivification are all presented as equivalents to deification. Although the concept itself is not controversial, Athanasius may well be intending to exclude any possibility of misunderstanding."[20] He expands the notion of *theōsis*, moving the emphasis away from immortality and incorruption to the exaltation of human nature through participation in the life of God. In Russell's words, "deification is certainly liberation from death and corruption, but it is also adoption as sons, the renewal of our nature by participation in the divine nature, a sharing in the bond of love of the Father and the Son, and finally entry into the kingdom of heaven in the likeness of Christ."[21]

With Cyril there is a development beyond Athanasius. For Cyril, we have a closer relationship to the whole Trinity, since he recognized strongly the indivisibility of the three persons in the one identical being of God.[22] Hence, in commenting on John 14:23, he states that the Holy Spirit is able to make us participants in the divine nature, since the Father, the Son, and the Spirit are one.[23] *Participation* is the key term throughout for Cyril, in keeping with the frequency with which he refers to 2 Peter 1:4, "partakers of the divine nature."[24] Only the Son is God by nature; we are children of God by participation.[25] Cyril approaches the matter theologically rather than mystically; we share in the life of Christ because Christ is "in us" and we are "in Christ."[26] His Christology stressed the unity of Christ. The eternal Word or Son is the subject of all Christ's actions. The humanity, which is complete— body and soul—is the humanity of the Word. Therefore, everything Jesus did was done by the eternal Son of God; Christ as the divine Son is the agent

---

19. Athanasius, *Serapion*, 1:24; *PG*, 26:584c.
20. Russell, *Deification*, 176–77.
21. Ibid., 178.
22. Ibid., 191–92.
23. Cyril of Alexandria, *Expositio Sive Commentarius in Ioannes Evangelium*, on John 14:23; *PG*, 74:291.
24. Russell, *Deification*, 192–94.
25. Cyril of Alexandria, *In Ioannes Evangelium*, lib. 11; *PG*, 74:541d.
26. Russell, *Deification*, 197.

of redemption.[27] His work of salvation is put into effect through the Holy Spirit, bringing about a dynamic relationship between us and God *through* the Spirit *in* Christ *with* the Father.[28] The incarnate Christ unites within himself the human and divine; he is united to God the Father because he is God by nature, and on the other hand he is united to human beings because he is truly human.[29] From our side, we are being transformed in the Eucharist. The Eucharist is filled with the energy of Christ, and so, when we participate in it, we are being changed, recovering the image and likeness of God.[30]

Russell sums up the Alexandrian teaching on *theōsis*:

> In summary, the Alexandrians used the metaphor of deification to indicate the glorious destiny awaiting human nature in accordance with the divine plan of salvation. The fundamental "moment" is the deification by the Logos of the representative human nature he received at the Incarnation. This has implications for individual human beings. The believer can participate in the deified flesh of Christ—the Lord's exalted humanity—through baptism, the Eucharist, and the moral life. Such participation leads to deification, not as a private mystical experience but as a transformation effected within the ecclesial body.[31]

Even in the strand of Eastern teaching exemplified by Maximus the Confessor, Russell concludes that he "is anxious to exclude both a Eutychian fusion of the divine and the human and an Origenistic ascent of the pure intellect to an undifferentiated assimilation to Christ. Deified human beings become god in the same measure that God became man, but although penetrated by divine energy they retain their created human status."[32]

Biblical Support for *Theōsis*

The overall biblical and theological context for our participation in the divine nature has been unfolded throughout the course of the book. If

27. Ibid., 198–99; Thomas G. Weinandy, "Cyril and the Mystery of the Incarnation," in *The Theology of St. Cyril of Alexandria: A Critical Appreciation*, ed. Thomas G. Weinandy and Daniel A. Keating (London: T&T Clark, 2003), 23–54.

28. Russell, *Deification*, 200–201; Cyril of Alexandria, *Dialogue on the Most Holy Trinity*, 7:639e–640e; *PG*, 75:1089.

29. Russell, *Deification*, 201.

30. Ibid., 202–3.

31. Ibid., 204.

32. Ibid., 193–94.

we are looking for specific biblical passages to support it, we could include everywhere that draws attention to the compatibility between God and man, to the incarnation, to Pentecost and the indwelling of the Holy Spirit, and to the transformation of believers into the image of Christ. In a number of passages, however, the theme comes to the surface in pronounced ways. Probably the first that springs to most minds is 2 Peter 1:3–4:

> His divine power has granted to us all things that pertain to life and godliness, through the knowledge of him who called us to his own glory and excellence, by which he has granted to us his precious and very great promises, so that through them you may become partakers of the divine nature. (ESV)

Through his precious and very great promises we become sharers of the divine nature (*theias koinōvoi phuseōs*)—this Peter presents as the goal of our calling by God. He has called us "to his own glory." Our destiny as Christians is to share the glory of God. It recalls Paul's comment that "all have sinned and fall short of the glory of God" (Rom. 3:23). Our proper place is to share God's glory; by sin we fell short and failed to participate in his glory, but in and through Christ we are restored to the glory of God as our ultimate destiny. Glory is what belongs distinctively and peculiarly to God. We are called to partake of what God is. This is more than mere fellowship. Fellowship entails intimate interaction but no participation in the nature of the one with whom such interaction takes place. Peter's language means that this goes far beyond external relations. It stops short of sharing in the being of God. There is an actual participation in the divine nature.[33] We will explore further what this may mean shortly.

John, in John 14:16ff., records Jesus' teaching that the Holy Spirit, on his coming at Pentecost, "will remain with you and shall be in you." In the presence of the Spirit, the *paraklētos*, Jesus himself was to be present (vv. 16–17). He then declares that for those who love him and keep his word, "my Father will love him and we shall come to him and take up our residence with him"

---

33. James Starr asks whether Peter relapses into Hellenistic dualism at this point. No, Starr concludes—he follows a Pauline and early Christian view of the world. Corruption is not the result of matter, but of sin. If deification is equality with God or absorption into the divine essence, Peter does not teach it. If, however, it is participation in and enjoyment of certain divine attributes, in part now and fully at Christ's return, the answer is yes, Peter does teach it. James Starr, "Does 2 Peter 1:4 Speak of Deification?" in *Partakers of the Divine Nature: The History and Development of Deification in the Christian Traditions*, ed. Michael J. Christensen and Jeffery A. Wittung (Grand Rapids: Baker Academic, 2007), 81–92.

(v. 23). The word *monē* means "a place where one may remain or dwell"[34] and conveys the idea of permanence.[35] The coming of the Holy Spirit is, in effect, the coming of the entire Trinity. The Father, the Son, and the Holy Spirit take up residence with the one who loves Jesus. This residence is permanent—the three remain with the faithful. It is of the greatest possible intimacy—the three indwell the one who loves Jesus. The faithful thus have a relation with the Trinity that is far, far closer than they enjoy with other human beings, no matter what relationship they may have with them. This goes beyond fellowship to communion (or participation) and is strictly a union, a joining together that is unbreakable.

Further, in 1 John 3:1–2, John writes:

> See what kind of love the Father has given to us, that we should be called children of God; and so we are. . . . Beloved, we are God's children now, and what we will be has not yet appeared; but we know that when he appears we shall be like him, because we shall see him as he is. (ESV)

The Father's love is such that we now share the relation to him that his Son has. We are now the children of God in Christ. Moreover, at his return, we will be transformed so as to be like Christ the Son. We will see him in his glory. We will share his glory. We will be in union with him.

Paul describes the Christian life as lived "in Christ" from beginning to end. This is clear in Ephesians 1, where the whole panorama of salvation from eternal election via redemption by the blood of Christ to our future inheritance is received in union with Christ. In 2 Corinthians 3:18 he writes of believers' being transformed from one degree of glory to another by the Spirit of the Lord. This surpasses the experience of Moses, whose face glowed after communing with Yahweh at Mount Sinai (2 Cor. 3:7–11).[36]

We refer to these few passages, but the whole tenor of Scripture points to such union. God has made us for this. He created us in Christ, the image of the invisible God. Following our sin, and the Son's redemptive work, we are

---

34. *LN*, 1:732.

35. Cf. *LS*, 2:1143.

36. Stephen Finlan says that it depends on what one means by *theōsis* as to whether Paul taught it. It cannot be separated from the sacrificial interchange associated with the death of Christ. He speaks of transformation, both progressive and eschatological, into the image of Christ. Stephen Finlan, "Can We Speak of *Theōsis* in Paul?" in *Partakers of the Divine Nature: The History and Development of Deification in the Christian Traditions*, ed. Michael J. Christensen and Jeffery A. Wittung (Grand Rapids: Baker Academic, 2007), 68–80.

being remade in the image of Christ. The Trinity created us with a capacity to live *in him*, as creatures in and with our Creator. The incarnation proves it. If it were not so and could not be so, then Jesus Christ—God and man—could not be one person, for the difference between Creator and creature would be so great that the incarnation would not be possible.

There are two decisive moments in this great and overwhelming sweep of God's purpose for us. First, in the incarnation the Son takes into personal union a single human nature. Second, the Holy Spirit comes at Pentecost and indwells or pervades myriads of human persons. There are clear differences here that reflect the differences between the persons of the Trinity. The Son unites a *single* human *nature*, while with the Spirit *countless* human *persons* are involved. With the Son there is a *personal union*, whereas the Spirit *pervades* or *indwells* us. These were the principal themes of chapters 2 and 3.

The Spirit, at Jesus' baptism, rested on him and led him in his subsequent faith, obedience, and ministry. In union with him, we are united with the Spirit who rests on him. The idea of indwelling denotes permanence, for he comes to remain in us forever. Yet the word could connote a certain incompleteness, as in the case of a liquid poured into a bucket, the bucket itself remaining unaffected, since the liquid merely fills the empty space. Pervasion, on the other hand, complements the image of indwelling by pointing to the idea of saturation, of thoroughness. Once more, this does not take away or diminish our humanity. After all, Jesus is fully and perfectly man—the most truly *human* man—and as such he is the Christ (the Anointed One) on whom the Spirit rests, directing him throughout the course of his life and ministry. Rather, pervasion by the Holy Spirit *establishes* our humanity.[37] He makes us what we ought to be. He frees us from the grip of a sinful, fallen nature and renews us to be like Christ. This is what it means to be human.[38] Well does Dumitru Staniloae comment when he affirms that only the Holy Trinity ensures our existence as persons, and that it is only because God is triune that salvation can occur.[39] Salvation not only reveals that God is triune but also proceeds from that reality.

---

37. This pervasion is somewhat akin to marriage, in which the two become one flesh. Marriage unites a man and a woman, but it does not diminish either one or eliminate their proper characteristics.

38. Incidentally, this is why naturalistic evolution is incompatible with the Christian faith, for man is made to be in union with God—in Christ and permeated by the Holy Spirit. This, not a particular exegesis of a single word in Genesis 1, utterly demarcates Christianity from evolutionism.

39. Dumitru Staniloae, *The Experience of God: Orthodox Dogmatic Theology*, vol. 1, *Revelation and Knowledge of the Triune God*, ed. and trans. Ioan Ionita and Robert Barringer (Brookline, MA: Holy Cross Orthodox Press, 1994), 276, 248.

In Nicolaus Cabasilas's words, as Christ flows into us and is blended with us, so he changes us and turns us to himself.[40] As Panayiotis Nellas comments, "The essence of the spiritual life is represented clearly by St. Paul's statement, 'It is no longer I who live but Christ who lives in me' (Gal. 2:20), provided that we take this statement in a literal sense." In fact, "the true nature of man consists in his being like God, or more precisely in his being like Christ and centered on Him."[41] In this, man's nature assumes the form of the deified humanity of Christ. This takes place not through the destruction of human characteristics but through their transformation.[42]

This is not pantheism, a breakdown of the Creator-creature distinction. It should not be understood to mean union with the essence of God. Nor is it some form of mixture of the divine and human, as advocated by some Eastern religions, in which both are like ingredients merged into an ontological soup. Rather, our humanity is not only preserved but enhanced. As Christ's humanity was not absorbed in the incarnation but retained its distinct integrity, so the Christian remains human. This union, not of nature but of grace, is so close that even our bodies are temples of the Holy Spirit (1 Cor. 6:19).

Again in Cabasilas's words, union with Christ "is closer than any other union which man can possibly imagine and does not lend itself to any exact comparisons." This is why, he says, Scripture does not confine itself to one illustration but provides a wide range of examples: a house and its occupants, wedlock, limbs and the head. Indeed, it is not possible to form an accurate picture even if we take all these metaphors together. For example, the limbs of Christ are joined more firmly to him than to their own bodies, for the martyrs laid down their heads and limbs with exultation and could not be separated from Christ even so far as to be out of earshot of his voice. In short, this union is closer than what joins a man to himself.[43] Again, the children of God are closer to Christ than to their own parents. Separated from our parents, we survive; separated from Christ, we would die.[44] Cabasilas urges constant meditation on Christ as a result of this, and has an extended series of meditations on the Beatitudes from a Christological perspective.[45]

---

40. Nicolaus Cabasilas, *Life in Christ*, trans. Margaret I. Lisney (London: Janus, 1995), 44.

41. Panayiotis Nellas, *Deification in Christ: Orthodox Perspectives on the Nature of the Human Person*, ed. Norman Russell (Crestwood, NY: St. Vladimir's Seminary Press, 1987), 120.

42. Ibid., 122–23.

43. Cabasilas, *Life in Christ*, 5–6.

44. Ibid., 48–49.

45. Ibid., 93–105.

This is a microcosm of the redemption of the whole created order. Christ, in his incarnation, took into union a centrally important part of this order. At the parousia the whole creation will be transformed and suffused with the glory of God. At the heart of all this is the redemption of the church and its own transformation in union with God. This does not mean that there is any possibility of sinless perfection in this life. Instead, it must be seen in tandem with the continued necessity of repentance and in conjunction with obedience to the commandments of God, participation in the life of the church, its ministry of word and sacrament, love to others, and care for the poor. It can no more conflict with justification than can sanctification and glorification, for it comes from the sheer grace of God as a priceless gift. There is a legal dimension to our salvation—God is righteous and salvation is in accordance with his law—and there is also a transformational dimension.[46]

How Far Was This Part of the Heritage of the Western Church?

Following Adolf von Harnack, it has been thought that this was an exclusively Eastern emphasis, alien to the Western church, which focused more heavily on the atonement and justification. Recent scholarship has undermined this thesis. Gerald Bonner has drawn attention to the theme in Augustine. Augustine, in sermon 192, echoes Athanasius and also refers to *theōsis* in his commentary on the Psalms, considering it to be an act of God's grace—by adoption, not generation—for it is the exact equivalent in Augustine's mind to adoption as sons.[47] In his sermon on Psalm 82 (81 in the original, following the accepted structure of the Psalms at the time), Augustine expounds these ideas. We were born to mortality, we endure infirmity, we look for divinity, for God wishes not only to give us life but also to deify us (*Gerimus mortalitatem, toleramus infirmitatem, exspectamus divinitatem. Vult enim Deus non solum vivificare, sed etiam deificare nos*). God made man, God was made man, and God will make us men gods. The Son of God was made the Son of Man that the sons of men might be made sons of God (*Filius Dei factus est filius hominis, ut filios hominum faceret filios*

---

46. For further reading on deification, see A. N. Williams, *The Ground of Union: Deification in Aquinas and Palamas* (New York: Oxford University Press, 1999); Carl Mosser, "The Greatest Possible Blessing: Calvin and Deification," *SJT* 55 (2002): 36–57; Emil Bartos, *Deification in Eastern Orthodox Theology: An Evaluation and Critique of the Theology of Dumitru Staniloae* (Carlisle, UK: Paternoster, 1999).

47. Gerald Bonner, "Deification, Divinization," in *Augustine through the Ages: An Encyclopedia*, ed. Allan D. Fitzgerald, OSA (Grand Rapids: Eerdmans, 1999), 265–66.

Dei). This does not mean, Augustine continues, that we undergo a change of substance. It is of a different manner, appropriate to creatures in contrast to the Creator.[48] The "gods" in this psalm are not gods by nature but by adoption and grace. There is only one true God, who is eternal, and who deifies. We worship God, who makes us gods.[49]

Anna Williams considers that the theme is present in Thomas Aquinas and compares his thought on the matter to that of his Eastern near-contemporary Gregory Palamas. In both cases, Thomas and Gregory agreed not only on the idea that salvation consists in becoming participants in the divine nature, but also on the theological factors that surround it. Both stringently maintain the distinction between Creator and creature, which they insist can never be breached. Humans remain human and are not changed into something other than what they are. Moreover, *theōsis* is—by definition—a gift from God. Only he can make us to share his nature. This of itself demonstrates that it is an act of grace, unearned and undeserved.[50] In Aquinas's case, it is part of a larger overall treatment of sanctification, the other parts having captured the attention of Western theologians. But "the West has no grounds for rejecting deification, not only because it can be found in Aquinas but also because it figures extensively in the patristic corpus and derives ultimately from scripture."[51] Williams continues, "East and West may thus be said to make different uses of the idea of *theōsis*, but this study indicates that at least until the Middle Ages, one cannot characterize the differences between East and West as deriving from two wholly divergent conceptions of either divinization or sanctification."[52] Williams's claims have come under criticism from Gösta Hallonstein, who points to a lack of clarity over what exactly Williams means by deification and also for her equating the *theme* of deification in Aquinas with the Eastern *doctrine* of deification in Palamas.[53]

This distinction of Hallonstein's between a theme and a doctrine is significant when it comes to the claims of the Finnish school of Luther

48. François Dolbeau, "Nouveaux Sermons de Saint Augustin Pour la Conversion Des Païens et Des Donatistes," *Revue des Études Augustiniennes* 39, 1 (1993): 97.

49. Ibid., 98.

50. In the case of Aquinas, see Williams, *The Ground of Union*, 34–101; in the case of Palamas, see ibid., 129–37.

51. Ibid., 174.

52. Ibid.

53. Gösta Hallonstein, "*Theōsis* in Recent Research: A Renewal of Interest and a Need for Clarity," in *Partakers of the Divine Nature: The History and Development of Deification in the Christian Traditions*, ed. Michael J. Christensen and Jeffery A. Wittung (Grand Rapids: Baker Academic, 2007), 281–93.

interpretation that Martin Luther's doctrine of justification by faith included *theōsis* as an integral part. This originated with Tuomo Mannermaa's claim that for Luther, Christ is not merely the object of faith but also its subject. Christ is present in the faith itself. He is the form of faith.[54] Moreover, God gives himself to us in his Word. "Faith means justification precisely on the basis of Christ's person being present in it as a favor and gift. *In ipsa fide Christus adest*: in faith itself Christ is present, and so the whole of salvation."[55] Here occasional comments by Luther are taken as if they were worked out systematically and developed to the status of constituent elements of his thought. That Luther on occasion sought to relate the forensic and transformational elements of salvation is hardly surprising; since both are integral to the Bible's teaching, this is something that most theologians will do. But to elevate such sporadic comments to the level of centrality in Luther's theology, often taken out of context, is at best misleading.[56] It is even more so when the passages are taken from the young Luther rather than from his more mature thought.[57] Steven Ozment argued persuasively that Luther, after 1518, showed little interest in the speculations of the German mystics in union with God.[58] Some of Mannermaa's critics, however, have not understood deification in Orthodox theology either, assuming that it entails ontological change, sharing the essence of God.

Reformed Theology on Union with Christ and Transformation

Reformed theology has generally used the term *union with Christ* to refer to this comprehensive sense of salvation, taking the form of both forensic and transformational elements. It is more Christocentric, in contrast to

54. Tuomo Mannermaa, "Justification and *Theōsis* in Lutheran-Orthodox Perspective," in *Union with Christ: The New Finnish Interpretation of Luther*, ed. Carl E. Braaten and Robert W. Jenson (Grand Rapids: Eerdmans, 1998), 25–41.

55. Tuomo Mannermaa, "Why Is Luther So Fascinating? Modern Finnish Luther Research," in *Union with Christ: The New Finnish Interpretation of Luther*, ed. Carl E. Braaten and Robert W. Jenson (Grand Rapids: Eerdmans, 1998), 14–15.

56. Further discussion of these themes in the Finnish school can be found in Robert W. Jenson, "Response to Mark Seifrid, Paul Metzger, and Carl Trueman on Finnish Luther Research," *WTJ* 65 (2003): 245–50; Paul Louis Metzger, "Mystical Union with Christ: An Alternative to Blood Transfusions and Legal Fictions," *WTJ* 65 (2003): 201–13; Mark A. Seifrid, "Paul, Luther, and Justification in Gal. 2:15–21," *WTJ* 65 (2003): 215–30; Carl R. Trueman, "Is the Finnish Line a New Beginning? A Critical Assessment of the Reading of Luther Offered by the Helsinki Circle," *WTJ* 65 (2003): 231–44.

57. Lowell C. Green, "Faith, Righteousness, and Justification: New Light on Their Development under Luther and Melanchthon," *SCJ* 4 (1972): 65–86.

58. Steven E. Ozment, *The Age of Reform 1250–1550* (New Haven: Yale University Press, 1980), 240–41.

Eastern pneumatocentrism.[59] Yet since Christ and the Holy Spirit work indivisibly and are, together with the Father, one being from eternity, it seems to me that, accordingly, theology has a responsibility to hold the work of Christ and the Holy Spirit together in unbroken union. This is also eminently biblical, since the gift of the Spirit was from the ascended and glorified Christ (John 7:37–39; 14:16–23; 16:8–11; Acts 2:33–36), the work of the Spirit is to testify of Christ (John 16:8–15), and the glorified Christ and the Holy Spirit are in the closest possible union in the thought of Paul (2 Cor. 3:17–18).[60]

We will now ask how classic Reformed theology understood the personal element of our union with Christ. In doing this, we will take more than a sidelong glance at how this relates to the question of our union with and transformation to be like God.

John Calvin

We will consider Calvin's statements chronologically, for there is a definite change in nuance at one point in his career. In the first edition of his *Institutes*, published in 1536, Calvin writes of union with Christ in terms of ingrafting into him in baptism. Paul does not exhort us to imitate Christ in his death and resurrection but says that through baptism we are made participants in his death so that we might be ingrafted in him (*nempe quod per baptismum Christus nos mortis suae fecerit participes, ut in eam inseramur*). We have the efficacy of his death and resurrection in the life-giving power of the Spirit (*simul etiam resurrectionis, in vivificatione spiritus*). Calvin cites Titus 3:5 in reference to baptism as the laver of regeneration and renewal. Baptism, Calvin says, is joined with repentance and regeneration in both John the Baptist and the apostles.[61]

In his Romans commentary of 1539, in dealing with Paul's argument in 6:5 he talks of Christ pouring his power into us, with the result that we share in his risen life, departing from our nature into his (*in eius naturam ex nostra demigramus*), the better nature of the Spirit renewing us.[62] According to Calvin, Paul means not only conformity to Christ's example but that secret union through which we are joined together with him, so that he invigorates

---

59. See Letham, *Through Western Eyes*, 243–65.

60. Vos argues that the phrases "in the Spirit" and "in Christ," when the latter is not used forensically, are equivalent in meaning in Paul's soteriology. Vos, *Pauline Eschatology*, 166.

61. *OS*, 1:129.

62. *CO*, 107; John Calvin, *Commentarius in Epistolam Pauli Ad Romanos, Ioannis Calvini Opera Omnia* (Genève: Librairie Droz, 1999), 121.

us by his Spirit and pours his power into us (*sed arcanam coniunctionem, per quam cum ipso coaluimus, ita ut nos Spiritu suo vegetans, eius virtutem in nos transfundat*). As the graft has the same life or death as the tree into which it is ingrafted, so we are partakers as much of the life as of the death of Christ (*ita vitae Christi non minus quam et mortis participes nos esse consentaneum est*).[63] The word *institii*, which translates the Greek *sumphutoi*—"united" (ESV), "be one with" (*LN*), "grown together" (*BDAG*)—has great *energia* or force, Calvin insists. Paul compares this union to a tree receiving sap from the root. There is, however, an evident disparity, Calvin comments, for the tree graft retains its natural quality in the fruit that is eaten. In spiritual ingrafting, on the other hand, not only do we derive the strength and sap of the life that flows from Christ, but we also pass from our nature into his (*sed in eius naturam ex nostra demigramus*). The efficacy of the death and resurrection of Christ renews in us the better nature of the Spirit (*alteram quoque resurrectionis, ad renovandam in nobis meliorem Spiritus naturam*).[64] Calvin here suggests that union with Christ entails a change in our nature. His nature, that of the Holy Spirit, replaces ours. Christ pours his life into us by the Spirit.

In his *Short Treatise on the Holy Supper of our Lord and Only Saviour Jesus Christ* (1540) and his Catechism of the Church of Geneva (1545), Calvin if anything takes this further. In the *Short Treatise* he concludes that "in receiving the sacrament in faith . . . we are truly made partakers of the real substance of the body and blood of Jesus Christ" and that "the Spirit of God is the bond of participation."[65] Moreover, "to deny the true communication of Jesus Christ to be offered to us in the Supper is to render this holy sacrament frivolous and useless."[66] In the Catechism he states that not only is the Lord's Supper a testimony of Christ's benefits or an exhibition of such things, but in it we are made partakers of Christ's substance as we are united with him (*je ne doute par qu'il ne nous face participans de sa propre substance, pour nous unir avec soy en une vie*). This he does "by the miraculous and secret virtue of his Spirit, for whom it is not difficult to associate things that are otherwise separated by an interval of space."[67]

---

63. *CO*, 49:107; Calvin, *Ad Romanos*, 120.

64. Calvin, *Ad Romanos*, 13:121.

65. John Calvin, *Calvin: Theological Treatises*, ed. J. K. S. Reid (Philadelphia: Westminster Press, 1954), 166.

66. Ibid., 146.

67. *CO*, 6:127–28; ibid., 137.

The following year, in his commentary on 1 Corinthians, Calvin reaffirms that in union with Christ we are given to share in his substance and life. In discussing 1 Corinthians 6:15, Calvin states that the spiritual union we have with Christ includes the body as well as the soul, so that we are flesh of his flesh, referencing Ephesians 5:30. The hope of the resurrection would be faint if our union with him were not complete and total like that.[68]

It is in his comments on Paul's discussion of the Lord's Supper in 1 Corinthians 11:24 that Calvin is most expansive. The first thing in union with Christ is that we are united to Christ himself; his benefits follow from the personal union that we are enabled to share (*Ego autem tunc nos demum participare Christi bonis agnosco, postquam Christum ipsum obtinemus*). We obtain Christ not so much when we believe he was sacrificed for us but when he dwells in us, when he is one with us, when we are members of his flesh, when we are joined together with him in one life and substance, Calvin considers (*sed dum in nobis habitat, dum est unum nobiscum, dum eius sumus membra ex carne eius, dum in unam denique et vitam et substantiam [ut ita loquor] cum ipso coalescimus*). Christ does not offer to us only the benefit of his death and resurrection but the same body in which he died and rose (*sed corpus ipsum, is quo passus est ac resurrexit*). That body is really (*realiter*) and truly (*vere*) given to us in the Supper, so that it may be health-giving food for our souls. Calvin draws to his clinching conclusion: "I mean that our souls are fed by the substance of his body, so that we are truly [*ut vere unum efficiamur cum eo*] made one with him; or, what amounts to the same thing, that a life-giving power from the flesh of Christ is poured into us through the medium of the Spirit, even though it is at a great distance from us, and is not mixed with us [*nec misceatur nobiscum*]."[69]

Hence, for Calvin union with Christ comes to particular expression in the Eucharist. Here we are fed with the body and blood of Christ. This is not corporeal, as Rome and the Lutherans held in very different ways, but is effected by the Holy Spirit. Christ has ascended to the right hand of God. His body is far from us spatially. But the Spirit unites things separated by distance, however great. In so doing, he enables us to feed on the glorified humanity of Christ. Until 1546, Calvin has not hesitated to say that we receive

---

68. John Calvin, *Calvin's Commentaries: The First Epistle of Paul the Apostle to the Corinthians*, trans. David W. Torrance and John W. Fraser (Grand Rapids: Eerdmans, 1960), 130.

69. Ibid., 246; *CO*, 49:487.

Christ's substance in union with him, seen in the Supper. He has even been prepared to state that we pass from our nature into his.

Two years later, in 1548, Calvin writes further on the theme in his Ephesians commentary. In dealing with the passage in chapter 5 where Paul compares the marriage relationship to that between Christ and the church, Calvin claims again that in union with Christ he communicates his substance to us. We grow into one body by the communication of his substance (*ita nos, ut simus vera Christi membra, substantiae eius communicare et hac communicatione nos coalescere in unum corpus*). In saying this, Paul testifies that we are of the members and bones of Christ (*Paulus nos ex membris et ossibus Christi esse testatur*). So, Calvin argues, in the Supper Christ offers his body to be enjoyed by us and to nourish us to eternal life (*corpus suum in Coena fruendum nobis exhibet, ut sit nobis vitae aeternae alimentum*).[70] On verse 31, Calvin states that "such is the union between us and Christ, that in a sense he pours himself into us [*se quodammodo in nos transfundit*]. We are bone of his bone because, by the power of his Spirit, he engrafts us into his body, so that from him we derive life [*Spiritus virtute nos in corpus suum inserit, ut vitam ex eo hauriamus*]."[71] We note the *quodammodo*—"in a sense" Christ pours himself into us. This alerts us to the possibility that Calvin is aware he is using language in a certain metaphorical manner, seeking to express in intelligible terms what transcends explanation. So much is evident when, in reaching verse 32, he acknowledges that this "is a great mystery . . . No language can do it justice . . . Whatever is supernatural is clearly beyond the grasp of our minds."[72]

This element of qualification surfaces again in Calvin's celebrated comments on 2 Peter 1:4, written in 1551, as it does in his writings after this date. In that chapter, we recall that Peter has said that God has given us his exceedingly great and precious promises, in order that, inter alia, "we might become partakers of the divine nature." Calvin recognizes the superlative nature of this gift, especially seeing the depths to which we had sunk in sin: "The excellence of the promises arises from the fact that they make us partakers of the divine nature, than which nothing more outstanding could be

---

70. John Calvin, *Calvin's Commentaries: The Epistles of Paul to the Galatians, Ephesians, Philippians and Colossians*, trans. T. H. L. Parker (Grand Rapids: Eerdmans, 1965), 208–9; John Calvin, *Commentarii in Pauli Epistolas, Ioannis Calvini Opera Omnia* (Genève: Librairie Droz, 1992), 16:272.

71. Calvin, *Epistles of Paul*, 209; Calvin, *In Pauli Epistolas*, 16:273.

72. Calvin, *Epistles of Paul*, 209–10; Calvin, *In Pauli Epistolas*, 16:273.

imagined" (*quo nihil praestantius cogitari potest*).[73] Indeed, "it is the purpose of the gospel to make us sooner or later like God; indeed, it is, so to speak, a kind of deification" (*Notemus ergo hunc esse Evangelii finem, ut aliquando conformes Deo reddamur; id vero est quasi deificari, ut ita loquamur*). He goes on to say that "nature" here does not mean "essence" but "kind"; we do not participate in the being of God but in his attributes, his qualities, for his nature refers to what he is like rather than who he is (*caeterum naturae nomen hic non substantiam sed qualitatem designat*).[74]

Garcia is wrong to rule out deification in Calvin—*quasi deificari* points in that direction. It stems from an apparent lack of familiarity on his part—in keeping with most other Calvin scholars—with the Eastern view of deification.[75] As we saw, Calvin's exposition here is quite compatible with what Athanasius or Cyril wrote. On the other hand, the *quasi* indicates a certain ambivalence by Calvin. From 1548, his comments are usually surrounded by a phrase such as "so to speak" (*ut ita loquor*), "in a certain way" (*quodammodo*), or the like. It is possible, of course, that Calvin was not entirely aware of the doctrine of *theōsis* in the Greek patristic tradition himself. While he mined the works of the fathers, he was dependent to a great extent on anthologies and used citations more as weapons in debate than as tools of a dispassionate historical theologian, if there is such a beast.[76]

On the other hand, Garcia may be right in suggesting that Calvin's thought on union with Christ underwent a development in the 1550s. He does not think it changed substantially but rather was enriched.[77] The qualification in his 2 Peter commentary is one matter. A new reticence seems to emerge

73. John Calvin, *Calvin's Commentaries: The Epistle of Paul the Apostle to the Hebrews and the First and Second Epistles of St. Peter*, trans. W. B. Johnston (Grand Rapids: Eerdmans, 1963), 330; John Calvin, *Commentarii in Epistolas Canonicas, Ioannis Calvini Opera Omnia* (Genève: Librairie Droz, 2009), 20:327.

74. Calvin, *Commentaries on Hebrews and 1&2 Peter*, 330; Calvin, *In Epistolas Canonicas*, 20:328.

75. This is evident in the lack in Garcia's bibliography of primary or secondary sources on the Greek patristic tradition. He assumes that the Eastern position necessarily entails a merging of divine and human, a participation in the essence of God. In fact, his otherwise outstanding exposition of Calvin's views is very close to what we have seen of the Alexandrian tradition of deification. See my remarks in note 122 below on the difference between Calvin and Osiander lying not in any denial of *theōsis* by Calvin but in his opposition to Osiander's claim of an *unmediated* infusion of the divine substance, Calvin agreeing on such participation on the basis that it happens by *the mediation of the incarnate flesh of Christ*. This insight was pointed out by a research student of mine, Andrew Ollerton. See Mark A. Garcia, *Life in Christ: Union with Christ and Twofold Grace in Calvin's Theology* (Milton Keynes, UK: Paternoster, 2008), 209f., 257–58.

76. Anthony N. S. Lane, *John Calvin: Student of the Church Fathers* (Grand Rapids: Baker, 1999), 67–86, 170–75, 232–34.

77. Garcia, *Life in Christ*, 210–11.

in his commentary on the Gospel of John, as well as in correspondence with Pietro Martire Vermigli, and while he develops his teaching on the Holy Spirit as the bond of union with Christ in his 1559 edition of the *Institutes*.

In the commentary on John, written in 1553, Calvin stresses that union with Christ transcends our mental capacities and is known only in faith, as the Holy Spirit pours into us the life of Christ. He refers to "the secret efficacy of the Spirit." We cannot know by idle speculation what is the sacred and mystic union between us and him and again between him and the Father (*qualis sit sacra et mystica inter nos et ipsum unio, qualis rursum inter ipsum et Patrem*), for the only way to know is when he pours his life into us by the secret efficacy of the Spirit (*quum vitam suam arcana Spiritus efficacia in nos diffundit*). This is the experience of faith.[78] Later, in commenting on John 17:21, he seems to contradict what he said in his Ephesians commentary and before. In this context, he denies that Christ transfuses his substance into us; instead, we receive his life, communicated to us by the Holy Spirit (*Unde etiam colligimus nos unum cum Christo esse, non quia suam in nos substantiam transfundat, sed quia Spiritus sui virtute nobiscum vitam suam et quicquid accepit a Patre bonorum communicet*).[79] This argues that Calvin actually backtracked after 1550. Whereas earlier he said on multiple occasions that we share in the substance of Christ, now he appears to deny it.

Two years later, in 1555, Calvin entered into an important exchange of letters with Pietro Martire Vermigli, the Italian Reformer, formerly based in Strasbourg and Oxford but now at Zurich. Vermigli wrote to Calvin on March 8 on "the communion we have with the body of Christ and the substance of his nature" (*de communione quam habemus cum corpore Christi atque substantia ipsius naturae*),[80] since it is a matter of great importance that the manner of our union with Christ be understood.[81] The chief benefit of the incarnation was that Christ chose to have communion with us in flesh and blood. Of itself, however, this is a very weak connection, since it entails communion by Christ with the whole human race. Something more is needed

---

78. John Calvin, *Calvin's Commentaries: The Gospel according to St. John 11–21 and the First Epistle of John*, trans. T. H. L. Parker (Grand Rapids: Eerdmans, 1959), 84; John Calvin, *In Evangelium Secundum Johannem Commentarius Pars Altera, Ioannis Calvini Opera Omnia* (Genève: Librairie Droz, 1998), 11, 2:150.

79. Calvin, *Gospel of John and 1 John*, 148; Calvin, *In Evangelium Johannem Pars Altera*, 11, 2:223.

80. English quotations from this correspondence are my translation.

81. *CO*, 15:494.

for reconciliation, a solid basis for forgiveness of sins and justification, which is provided by the Holy Spirit, who makes us capable of immortality and conforms us more and more to Christ by breathing faith into us. This is union with Christ effected by the Spirit through faith.[82] This involves no change in our nature. We do not change into the body and flesh of Christ (*Non quod substantiam suae naturae abiiciant, et re ipsa in corpus atque carnem Christi transeant*), for it is a spiritual communion by which we are renewed from regeneration to glorification (*vero contingit per Christi spiritum quo ab ipsa regeneratione ad speciem eius gloriae innovamur*).[83] There is a third form of communion, which actually precedes this spiritual one. It occurs when we believe and Christ becomes our head and we his members.[84] This happens secretly (*haec illa est arcana communio qua illi dicimur inseri*).[85]

On August 8, 1555, Calvin replied, indicating his full agreement with Vermigli.[86] While this concord extended to Vermigli's threefold classification, Calvin focuses on the intermediate element of union, by which we are joined to Christ as our head. He writes of the communion in which we are joined together with him in one body (*et facit ut in unum cum ipso corpus coalescamus*).[87] We are made his members, and life flows to us from the head; there is no other way we can be reconciled by his sacrificial death than that by which he is ours and we are one with him (*Neque enim aliter nos Deo mortis suae sacrificio reconciliat, nisi quia noster est ac nos unum cum ipso*).[88] This union is stronger and closer than merely fellowship (*consortis*) or affinity, association, or partnership (*societatis*), for it is a sacred unity "by which the Son of God ingrafts us into one body and communicates to us all his things. So we drink life from his flesh and blood, so that it is not inappropriately called nourishment."[89] Calvin precludes "a crass mixture of substances," for it is enough that Christ is in heavenly glory and that life from him flows to us. It is absurd to think that Christ and we become one essence. On the other hand, Calvin recognizes, union with Christ is beyond our understanding (*Quomodo id fiat, intelligentiae meae modulo longe altius esse fateor*).[90]

82. Ibid.
83. Ibid.
84. Ibid.
85. Ibid., 15:495.
86. Ibid., 15:724.
87. Ibid., 15:722–23.
88. Ibid., 15:723.
89. Ibid.
90. Ibid.

In the following year, 1556, Calvin wrote his *Secunda defensio piae et orthodoxae de sacramentis fidei, adversus Joachimi Westphali calulmnias*. Here he wrote that the soul has no less communion in the blood of Christ than wine with the mouth when we drink (*nec minus sanguinis communionem anima percipiat, quam ore vinum bibimus*).[91]

In 1559 came the final Latin edition of Calvin's *Institutes*. Here he made plain the connection between the work of Christ and that of the Holy Spirit. "First, we must understand that as long as Christ remains outside of us, and we are separated from him, all that he has suffered and done for the salvation of the human race remains useless and of no value to us." All that Christ possesses "is nothing to us until we grow into one body with him." It is through "the secret energy of the Spirit, by which we come to enjoy Christ and all his benefits," for "the Holy Spirit is the bond by which Christ effectively joins us to himself."[92] For Calvin, Christ's work benefits us only when we are united to him. Union with Christ is the root of salvation, justification and sanctification included. This occurs through faith, but faith itself is the fruit of the Holy Spirit's work. So the Spirit unites us to Christ. First, the Father bestowed the whole fullness of the Spirit on Christ in a special way, so as to gather his people to the hope of the eternal inheritance.[93] Faith is the principal work of the Holy Spirit,[94] occurring in our being united to Christ: "For we await salvation from him not because he appears to us afar off, but because he makes us, ingrafted into his body, participants not only in all his benefits but also in himself."[95] If we were to contemplate ourselves, it would be sure damnation. "But since Christ has been so imparted to you with all his benefits that all his things are made yours, that you are made a member of him, indeed one with him, his righteousness overwhelms your sins; his salvation wipes out your condemnation." So "we ought not to separate Christ from ourselves or ourselves from him." As a result, "Christ is not outside us but dwells within us. Not only does he cleave to us by an indivisible bond of fellowship, but with a wonderful communion, day by day, he grows more and more into one body with us, until he becomes completely one with us."[96]

91. Ibid., 9:65.
92. *Institutes*, 3.1.1.
93. Ibid., 3.1.2.
94. Ibid., 3.1.4.
95. Ibid., 3.2.24.
96. Ibid.

In terms of justification, this means that we are righteous only in Christ.[97] In this sense, union with Christ has priority to justification by faith. It is only as we are united with Christ that God accounts us righteous.

> Therefore, that putting together of Head and members, that indwelling of Christ in our hearts—in short, that mystical union—are accorded by us the highest degree of importance, so that Christ, having been made ours, makes us sharers with him in the gifts with which he has been endowed. We do not, therefore, contemplate him outside ourselves from afar in order that his righteousness may be imputed to us but because we put on Christ and are engrafted into his body—in short, because he deigns to make us one with him. For this reason, we glory that we have fellowship of righteousness with him.[98]

Precisely because righteousness is imputed to us because we are one with Christ—brought about by the Holy Spirit through faith—it is Christ's righteousness that is ours. "You see that our righteousness is not in us but in Christ, that we possess it only because we are partakers of Christ."[99] Since "all his things are ours and we have all things in him, in us there is nothing."[100] As soon as we are engrafted into Christ through faith, we are made sons of God, heirs of heaven, possessors of life and all the merits of Christ.[101] Thus, we receive both justification and sanctification in union with Christ, both at the same time, for Christ cannot be divided into pieces. We cannot possess Christ without at the same time being made partakers in his sanctification.[102] We have no hope of our future inheritance unless we have been united to Christ. The elect are so united to Christ that they have been called to participate in one God and Christ (*in unius Dei ac Christi participationem etiam vocati*).[103]

Therefore, according to Calvin, in the sacraments the benefits are conferred by Christ alone through the Holy Spirit, who makes us participants in Christ (*per Spiritum sanctum, qui nos facit Christi ipsius participes*).[104] Through baptism, the laver of regeneration, Christ makes us to share in his

---

97. Ibid., 3.11.8; *OS*, 4:190.
98. *Institutes*, 3.11.10; *OS*, 4:191.
99. *Institutes*, 3.11.23; *OS*, 4:206–7.
100. *Institutes*, 3.15.5; *OS*, 4:245.
101. *Institutes*, 3.15.6; *OS*, 4:245.
102. *Institutes*, 3.16.1; *OS*, 4:248–49.
103. *Institutes*, 4.1.2; *OS*, 5:4.
104. *Institutes*, 4.14.16; *OS*, 5:274.

death that we may be ingrafted in it.[105] So baptism is a token of our union with Christ.[106] Christ by sharing in our human mortality made us partakers in his divine immortality, raising our corruptible flesh to glory and incorruption (*quum humanae nostrae mortalitatis participes factus nos divinae suae immortalitatis consortes fecit*).[107] This is applied to us through the gospel but even more clearly through the sacred Supper, in which the soul most truly and deeply becomes partaker of Christ. So his life passes into us and is made ours (*ut vita sua in nos transeat*), just as bread taken as food imparts vigor to the body.[108] Calvin explains how this happens:

> We can explain the nature of this by a familiar example. Water is sometimes drunk from a spring, sometimes drawn, sometimes led by channels to water the fields, yet it does not flow forth from itself for so many uses, but from the very source, which by unceasing flow supplies and serves it. In like manner, the flesh of Christ is like a rich and inexhaustible fountain that pours into us the life springing forth from the Godhead into itself. Now who does not see that communion of Christ's flesh and blood is necessary for all who aspire to heavenly life?[109]

This communion is achieved by the Holy Spirit. Even though it seems unbelievable, since Christ's flesh is separated from us by such a great distance, "the secret power of the Holy Spirit towers above all our senses" and "truly unites things separated by distance" in the Supper.[110] The bond of this connection is, then, the Spirit of Christ, "with whom we are joined in unity" and who "is like a channel through which all that Christ himself is and has is conveyed to us." It is the Spirit who imparts to us the communion of his flesh and blood. "On this account, Scripture, in speaking of our participation with Christ, relates its whole power to the Spirit."[111]

Finally, in his treatise opposing the Lutheran Tileman Heshus, *The clear explanation of sound doctrine concerning the true partaking of the flesh and blood of Christ in the Holy Supper*, written in 1561, Calvin sums up and expands his thesis. He says, "When I say that the flesh and blood of Christ

---

105. *Institutes*, 4.15.5; *OS*, 5:288.
106. *Institutes*, 4.15.6; *OS*, 5:289.
107. *Institutes*, 4.17.4; *CO*, 5:345.
108. *Institutes*, 4.17.5; *CO*, 5:346–47.
109. *Institutes*, 4.17.9; *OS*, 5:350–51.
110. *Institutes*, 4.17.10; *OS*, 5:351–52.
111. *OS*, 5:355–56; *Institutes*, 4.17.12.

are substantially offered and exhibited to us in the Supper, I at the same time explain the mode, namely, that the flesh of Christ becomes vivifying to us, inasmuch as Christ, by the incomprehensible virtue of his Spirit, transfuses his own proper life into us from the substance of his flesh, so that he himself lives in us, and his life is common to us."[112] The mode of communication Calvin claims is "that Christ by his boundless and wondrous powers unites us into the same life with himself, and not only applies the fruit of his passion to us, but becomes truly ours by communicating his blessings to us, and accordingly joins us to himself, as head and members unite to form the body. I do not restrict this union to the divine essence, but affirm that it belongs to the flesh and blood."[113] He argues that "this flesh of ours which he assumed is vivifying for us, so that it becomes the material of spiritual life for us," while it is a mystery that transcends our mental powers.[114] There is no need for Christ's body to undergo any change of place, "since by the secret virtue of the Spirit he infuses his life into us from heaven . . . since the efficacy of the Spirit surmounts all natural obstacles."[115] This is so because Calvin "[asserts] a substantial communion" and discards only a local presence as in the Lutheran claim.[116] This is nothing additional to the gospel; rather, the Supper seals what is offered in the gospel.[117]

Carl Mosser has argued that Calvin teaches a doctrine of deification.[118] He was strongly opposed by Jonathan Slater,[119] but from assumptions akin to Nestorianism. Slater considers that Calvin treats the humanity of Christ as effectively autonomous; this precludes any idea of deification. In this, Slater's interpretation of Calvin is suspect. His citations of Calvin are limited to the *Institutes*. Moreover, the theological parameters on which he bases his claims are unsustainable. His Calvin is quasi-Nestorian, and it appears that Slater shares these thoughts himself. Nestorius had no doctrine of deification, of course, since he held the two natures of Christ apart. Slater treats the human nature of Christ by itself and argues that Calvin does so, too. The price for this is the jeopardizing of the unity of the person of Christ. It indicates that

112. Calvin, *Theological Treatises*, 267.
113. Ibid., 268.
114. Ibid.
115. Ibid., 278.
116. Ibid., 287.
117. Ibid., 281.
118. Mosser, "Calvin and Deification."
119. Jonathan Slater, "Salvation as Participation in the Humanity of the Mediator in Calvin's Institutes of the Christian Religion: A Reply to Carl Mosser," *SJT* 58 (2005): 39–58.

objections to *theōsis* stem largely from a correct stress on the Creator-creature distinction at the expense of their compatibility.[120] This tendency yields a Nestorian Christology in which deity and humanity are kept separate, the unity of Christ's person—and the incarnation itself—undermined, and so his achievement of redemption jeopardized.[121]

It seems to me that until around 1550 Calvin had some strong language about our participation in the substance of Christ's flesh, Christ pouring his life into us by the Holy Spirit, and wrote of our nature being changed. He states on several occasions that Christ pours his substance into us. After that time, he seems to qualify those terms and to distance himself from the idea that somehow Christ's substance was in any way transmitted to us by the Holy Spirit in the Eucharist. Yet this does not diminish his recognition that this is a mystery that transcends our capacities to fully grasp. Nor does it undermine his point that we are united with the saving humanity of Christ; it is a difference of tone rather than substance. During this time he was faced by controversies with a range of Lutherans, particularly Osiander with his claim that we are righteous by the divine righteousness of Christ, indwelling essentially in us.[122] Ultimately, Calvin's most frequent imagery becomes that of the Holy Spirit uniting us to Christ through faith, and so the *life* of Christ—the risen and ascended Christ—is given to us to nourish us, particularly in the Lord's Supper.[123] At the root of this is that Christ has

---

120. See chapter 1.

121. At times, however, Calvin's own Christology raises questions. In his comments on 1 Corinthians 15:27–28, he states that Christ will hand the kingdom from his humanity to his divinity (as if the two were separable). Moreover, Christ's humanity keeps us from a nearer vision of God, and so in glorification it will no longer be between us and God. This more than suggests that Calvin viewed the two natures in such distinction as to verge on separation. He seems to suggest the same thing in *Institutes*, 2.14.3. This may explain his own equivocation on deification. It is in striking contrast to his correct teaching that Christ's humanity, far from keeping us from God, is the means by which we come to know him. In fact, in the context of 2.14.3–4, Calvin clearly opposes Nestorius, so we must conclude that his statements in these places were untypically careless. See Yang-Ho Lee, "Calvin on Deification: A Reply to Carl Mosser and Jonathan Slater," *SJT* 63 (2010): 272–84, for an analysis of both Mosser and Slater, in which he attempts to correct the imbalances he perceives them to have.

122. Osiander published his *Disputation on Justification* in 1550, the year after Calvin and Heinrich Bullinger reached an agreement on the sacraments, in the *Consensus Tigurinus*, in response to the *Augsburg Interim* of 1548, which parceled out political jurisdictions in Europe between Roman Catholics and Lutherans, leaving the Reformed isolated. See the new section in the 1559 *Institutes*, 3.5–11, written expressly to counter Osiander. Here, as one of my research students, Andrew Ollerton, has pointed out to me, Calvin opposes Osiander's claim on the unmediated infusion of divine substance with his own position on mediation of the divine nature through the incarnate flesh of Christ, a point that Calvin scholars have generally missed.

123. On Calvin and the Lord's Supper, see B. A. Gerrish, *Grace and Gratitude: The Eucharistic Theology of John Calvin* (Minneapolis: Fortress Press, 1993); Thomas J. Davis, *The Clearest Promises of God:*

become one with us in the incarnation, and consequently his flesh receives the life of the Godhead poured into it. From this we receive life in union with him. Together with his concern for the integrity of the humanity of Christ, this leads him to couch his language on themes such as deification in such terms as *quasi* ("a kind of"), *ita ut loquor* ("so to speak"), and *quodammodo* ("in a certain manner"). In this he opposes the Lutheran view of the *communicatio idiomatum* ("communication of idioms") in which attributes of Christ's deity are transmitted to his humanity. This appeared to blur the distinction between the two and, in the eyes of the Reformed, undermined the humanity. He was not dealing with the Eastern position; in fact, it was the Lutherans who were the innovators, and Calvin was closer to the East than many have realized. I suggest that the pressure from Lutheran apologists and the need to conciliate Zurich after 1548 may have tempered his language, rather than substantially altering his doctrine.

Amandus Polanus (1561–1610)

We now turn our attention to a significant theologian from the late sixteenth and early seventeenth centuries. Polanus was more a consolidator of Reformed doctrine than an innovator and, for that reason, is representative of how Reformed theology stood at that time.[124] Among his works is a handbook of doctrine, *Partitiones Theologicae*, first published at Basel in 1586. It was followed in 1609 by a far more extensive and detailed work, the *Syntagma Christianae Theologiae*. In the *Partitiones*, Polanus takes a much weaker position than Calvin, but in the *Syntagma* he develops his thought on union with Christ to a much greater extent, approaches Calvin's teaching, and in some ways goes beyond it.

The Development of Calvin's Eucharistic Teaching (New York: AMS Press, 1995); Thomas J. Davis, *This Is My Body: The Presence of Christ in Reformation Thought* (Grand Rapids: Baker Academic, 2008), 65–90, 127–48; Ronald S. Wallace, *Calvin's Doctrine of the Word and Sacrament* (Edinburgh: Oliver and Boyd, 1953); Keith A. Mathison, *Given for You: Reclaiming Calvin's Doctrine of the Lord's Supper* (Phillipsburg, NJ: P&R Publishing, 2002), 3–48; Robert Letham, *The Lord's Supper: Eternal Word in Broken Bread* (Phillipsburg, NJ: P&R Publishing, 2001), 31–37.

124. See Robert Letham, "Amandus Polanus: A Neglected Theologian?" *SCJ* 21 (1990): 463–76; Muller calls him "a theologian of considerable stature." Richard A. Muller, *Christ and the Decree: Christology and Predestination in Reformed Theology from Calvin to Perkins* (Grand Rapids: Baker, 1986), 130. Muller also calls him "the most compendious systematic theologian of the early orthodox period" of Reformed scholasticism. Richard A. Muller, *After Calvin: Studies in the Development of a Theological Tradition* (Oxford: Oxford University Press, 2003), 148.

In the *Partitiones*, Polanus stresses the elevation of the humanity assumed by Christ in the incarnation. The effects of the personal union in Christ are twofold: the exaltation of the assumed human nature to the highest and ineffable dignity (rank) and the communication of idioms (*exaltatio naturae assumtae ad summam & ineffabilem dignitatem & communicatio idiomatum*). This exaltation entails the honor that the person of Christ communicates to the assumed nature; it is exalted above all angels and men. It consists in personal union with the Logos (*quia humana natura in unitatem personae filii Dei est assumta: ita ut sit caro propria aeterni Filii Dei, Heb.2.16*). Hence, the Son raises the assumed humanity to the highest status precisely in the personal union that took place. Moreover, the Holy Spirit gave the greatest fullness of gifts that it is possible for a human nature to have, not only in number but in *excellentisimus gradae*. In this, Polanus recognizes, as the Greeks and Calvin did, the effect of the incarnational union on the assumed humanity of Christ.[125]

Polanus connects our own union with Christ with the sacraments, as Calvin did. In communion with Christ, he gives us eternal life. Polanus produces a range of biblical terms to describe this union. It is said to be a joining, a union, a coalescence, ingrafting in Christ, eating the flesh and drinking the blood of Christ (in the Lord's Supper), being brought under one head, our joining together in one body under one head, cleansing with the blood of Christ, vivification, our being raised from the dead, and our placement in heaven as one with Christ.[126] Polanus considers that communion with Christ embraces justification and regeneration, adoption, and the liberties of the sons of God.[127] When he discusses the Lord's Supper, however, he focuses on our participation in the benefits of the covenant of grace—reconciliation, justification, regeneration—so that, in effect, we feed on justification rather than Christ himself.[128]

In the *Syntagma* (1609), he goes much further. Polanus writes of communion with Christ as a union in which Christ and we are really and truly joined and remain so forever (*Communio ipsiusmet Christi, est unio*

---

125. Amandus Polanus, *Partitiones Theologicae*, 2nd ed. (Basel, 1590), 59–60.

126. "Ea dicitue etiam conjunctio, unio, coalitio cum Christi, insitio in Christum, manducatio carnis Christi, bibito sanguinis Christi, *Anakephalaiōsis*, id est, reductio sub unum caput, conjunctio in unum corpus sub uno capito Christi. Ephes.1.10. Ablutio sanguine Christi, vivificatio nostri, excitatio nostri ex mortuis, collocatio nostri in coelis unam cum Christo." Ibid., 82–83.

127. Ibid., 84–85.

128. Ibid., 127.

ipsius nobiscum, qua nos sibi vere & realiter copulavit ut ipse in nobis & nos in ipso maneamus in sempiternam).[129] This has a threefold form: first, in nature, in the incarnation; second, in grace, in the elect; and third, after this life, when we are present with the Lord.[130] The first occurs through the assumption of our nature in the unity of Christ's person. The second is through Christ's assumption of our persons, not in one person with him but in grace (*per assumtionem personarum nostrarum non quidem in unam eum ipso personam: sed in gratiam*). He is the head; we are members of his body, of his flesh and bones. So we partake of his divine nature, as Peter says (*ex carne eius, & ex ossibus eius: adeoque in participationem naturae ipsius divinae, ut Petrus loquitur. 2 Petr.1. vers.4*).[131] The third form is the assumption of our nature with him in eternal glory. There is a progression from the first to the second to the third, from nature to grace to glory. Each stage is the cause of the next.[132] The efficient cause is the most blessed and holy Trinity. This includes the Son's assumption of our nature through Mary, the Father daily uniting his elect to his Son by the Holy Spirit and, at the last day, raising us from the dead through the Son by the Holy Spirit.[133] The ministerial cause of our union with Christ is the gospel and saving faith.[134]

Polanus then discusses *what* our union with Christ actually is. It is not imaginary, for it is true and real (*vere ac realis*). It is also indissoluble.[135] It is here that Polanus goes as far as Calvin ever went, if not further. This union, he says, *is essential*. We exist in our earthly bodies but with the divine nature of Christ dwelling in us. According to his humanity he is in heaven, but the same Holy Spirit who remains in us and in him joins us together, no less than the members of our bodies are joined. Consequently, this union consists not only in the communication of gifts but also of the substance of Christ. The union, then, is substantial, actual, and corporeal. The manner of union is, of course, spiritual. But it is substantial and corporeal in terms of the subjects united, since it is true substance and nature, his body and our nature, that are related or

---

129. Amandus Polanus, *Syntagma Theologiae Christianae* (Geneva: Petri Auberti, 1612), 2:330b.
130. Ibid., 2:330e.
131. Ibid., 2:330e–f.
132. Ibid., 2:330g.
133. Ibid., 2:330g–331c.
134. Ibid., 2:331c.
135. Ibid., 2:331g–h.

akin (*affine*); and we are truly joined to the substance and both natures of Christ and thus to his body.[136]

Polanus goes on to explain how we are united to Christ according to both natures. Citing 2 Peter 1:4, he points out that Christ dwells in us according to his divine nature and makes us conformable to him (*ipse sua Deitate reipsa in nobis habitat & nos sibi conformes redit. 2 Pet.1.4*).[137] We also have communion with Christ according to his human nature. We participate according to nature—our nature is to be conformed to Christ by sanctification of the Holy Spirit. We also participate in the Holy Spirit, who joins us to the Lord. (*Qui agglutinatur Domino, unus cum eo Spiritus est.*)[138]

The Holy Spirit unites us to Christ in the sacraments.[139] The sacramental union is spiritual, with a conjunction between the sign (*signum*) and the thing signified (*res*). The bread and wine we see with bodily eyes; the body and blood we see with the eyes of the soul, which is faith.[140] The body of Christ is in heaven corporeally. To us it is on the earth (*in terra*), spiritually present by means of the Holy Spirit, who dwells in Christ and in us and unites us to the head as members (*mediante Spiritu suo in illo & in nobis habitante*). The body of Christ is absent *in loco* but most present to us by our union with him, through the Spirit of Christ, who dwells in him and in us (*sed praesentissimus est nobis unione nostri cum illo, per habitantem in eo & in nobis Christi Spiritum*).[141] Consequently, we are united to Christ through the Holy Spirit and through faith.[142] Therefore, the bread and wine are signs not only signifying but also *exhibiting* (*Unde panis & vinum non tantum significativa signa sunt, sed etiam exhibitiva*). Therefore, Christ with and in these signs exhibits his body and blood and thus truly gives the Holy

---

136. "Eadem unio est *essentialis*: quia nos licet in terris corporibus nostris & substantia animae exsistentes, tamen & cum divina Christi natura in nobis habitante, & cum humana, quam iam in coelo est, per eundem Spiritum Sanctum in illa & in nobis manentem vere copulamur, non minus quam per animam capiti brachia, tibiae, pedes & reliqua membra corporis coniunguntur: ac proinde non tantum donorum, sed etiam substantiae Christi communicatione unio haec constat." The union is substantial, actual, and corporeal: not in terms of its manner, which is spiritual, but in respect of the subjects or objects united, since that is true substance and nature, his body and our nature *affine*; and we are truly joined to the substance and both natures of Christ and thus to his body: "sed respectu subiecti seu obiecti cum unimur, quia illud est vera substantia & natura, verum ipsius corpus & nostrae naturae affine: & substantiae & naturae Christi utrique atque sic & corpori eius vere iungimur." Polanus, *Syntagma*, 2:332b–c.

137. Ibid., 2:332d.
138. Ibid., 2:332e–f.
139. Ibid., 2:434a–b.
140. Ibid., 2:455c–d.
141. Ibid., 2:455e.
142. Ibid., 2:455h.

Spirit to his disciples. The manner of the presence of the body and blood of Christ is therefore sacramental and spiritual.[143] Polanus therefore argues for a substantial union with Christ that comes to expression especially in the Lord's Supper.

Rowland Stedman (1630?–73)

A book of major significance for union with Christ, and its personal dimensions, was written and published in 1668 by Rowland Stedman, one of the ministers ejected from their livings in 1662. Stedman points to the biblical imagery that expresses this union. First, there is *a natural analogy*, between the head and members of the body. In this sense, Christ is the head of his church, an intimate union; as the members of the body are animated with the same soul, so the church is given life by the Spirit of the Son. Second, there is *a corporal analogy*, that of the vine and the branches. As the branches depend on the sap that rises through the plant, so Christ is the root from which all is derived, the whole depending on him for life. Third is *a conjugal analogy*, as of a husband and wife. The marriage union means the two become one flesh. In turn, Christ and the church are united as one spirit, as Paul says in Ephesians 5:31–32. Fourth comes *an artificial analogy* of a building and its foundation, such as Paul makes in 1 Corinthians 3:9–11. Christ in this sense is both the doctrinal and personal foundation of the church and its members.[144] Note that in each of Stedman's analogies the respective parts retain their particular distinctiveness. The husband and wife remain husband and wife, while becoming one flesh. The branches remain branches, while being part of a much larger whole. The head remains the head and the members remain members, while joined in one united organism. In fact, the parts could not be what they are if detached from that to which they are united and that which gives them their distinctive identity as parts of a whole. Moreover, we can suppose from these analogies that because they point to a greater reality, our union with Christ is greater, closer, and more secure than any of them taken singly or together.[145]

143. Ibid., 2:456d.
144. Rowland Stedman, *The Mystical Union of Believers with Christ, or A Treatise Wherein That Great Mystery and Priviledge of the Saints Union with the Son of God Is Opened* (London: W. R. for Thomas Parkhurst, at the Golden-Bible on London-Bridge, under the gate, 1668), 239–60, Wing / 335:13.
145. Nellas, *Deification in Christ*, 119.

Union with Christ and the Sacraments

The central affirmation of the chapter on the Lord's Supper in the WCF is that the faithful, or "worthy receivers," "receive and feed upon Christ" (WCF 29.7). They are enabled to do this really and truly; it is no fiction, for the sacraments are more than merely symbolic. On the other hand, this feeding is spiritual, not corporeal, and so depends on the Holy Spirit and requires faith on our part. The Assembly set its face against the Roman Catholic doctrine of the sacraments working *ex opere operato*, by the fact of being performed. In keeping with the Reformed tradition, however, the divines were equally opposed to the Anabaptist claim that they were simply symbols and memorials. Earlier, John Knox had strongly rebutted these notions in the Scots Confession (1560): "And this we utterlie damne the vanitie of thay that affirme Sacramentes to be nathing ellis bot naked and baire signes. No, wee assuredlie beleeve that be Baptisme we ar ingrafted in Christ Jesus, to be made partakers of his justice, be quhilk our sinnes ar covered and remitted."[146] Hence, for the Reformed, the sacraments are signs and seals of the covenant of grace, exhibiting the grace signified, which grace is conferred by the Holy Spirit in his own time and manner to those for whom it applies (WCF 27.3; 28.6). Baptism exhibits our ingrafting into Christ, in regeneration, justification, sanctification, and so on, which the Spirit confers in due time. In the Lord's Supper Christ gives himself for us to feed us and nourish us to everlasting life.

This is a contrast to the objectivity of Lutheranism, in which the sacraments are efficacious unless resisted. For Lutherans, in the Lord's Supper the body and blood of Christ are held to be corporeally present in, with, and under the bread and wine. In contrast, the Reformed insist that the feeding is spiritual, in and by the Holy Spirit, and received in faith. The efficacious working of the Holy Spirit is not tied to place or time. As the WCF claims, the grace signified and exhibited is conferred by the Holy Spirit in his own time to those to whom it belongs—the elect. Grace is not automatic.

This is also in contrast to the neo-Zwinglianism of William Cunningham, Robert L. Dabney, and latterly Wayne Spear.[147] The sacraments are more

---

146. Philip Schaff, *The Creeds of Christendom* (Grand Rapids: Baker, 1966), 3:467–70.

147. Wayne Spear, "The Nature of the Lord's Supper according to Calvin and the Westminster Assembly," and "Calvin and Westminster on the Lord's Supper: Exegetical and Theological Considerations," in *The Westminster Confession into the 21st Century: Essays in Rememberance [Sic] of the 350th Anniversary of the Westminster Assembly*, vol. 3, ed. J. Ligon Duncan III (Fearn, Ross-shire, UK: Mentor, 2009), 355–414.

than symbolic, although they have symbolism aplenty. The Supper is more than a sign and seal of the covenant of grace. It exhibits the grace of union with Christ, from regeneration to glorification; in the seventeenth century, *exhibit* was a stronger word than it is today, carrying a connotation close to *confer*. Moreover, the grace exhibited is also conferred not by the sacrament itself but by the Holy Spirit (WCF 27.3; 28.1, 6; 29.7). The Supper is the *koinōnia* of the body and blood of Christ (1 Cor. 10:16–17).

John W. Nevin and Charles Hodge

In nineteenth-century America, John W. Nevin, when he was on the faculty of Mercersburg Seminary from 1840 to 1853, brought these questions to the forefront when opposing the individualism and nonchurchly direction of American Protestantism. In particular, his book *The Mystical Presence* sought to recover the Reformed doctrine of the Eucharist. He followed in 1850 with a 128-page article in the *Mercersburg Review* developing his historical argument at length, a piece of research that stood for a century. Nevin argued that the Reformed churches of his day had deviated from the classic confessions, reduced the sacrament to mere symbolism and memorialism, and viewed our relationship with Christ in external and contractual terms only.[148]

For Nevin, salvation in Christ consists of a new life, the life of Christ located in his people, the church. Our relationship with Christ is deep and personal, going far beyond anything known to Adam. This mystical union is with the *person* of Christ and thus with his humanity, which can never be severed from the personal union into which it was assumed in the incarnation. This union is not corporeal but spiritual—yet it is nonetheless real, effected by the Holy Spirit through faith. It comes to expression in the Holy Supper, in which we have a real communication with the person of Christ under the form of a sacramental mystery.[149] For Nevin, our participation in Christ entails the reception of his life, which is expressed in the church. It

---

148. John Williamson Nevin, *The Mystical Presence: A Vindication of the Reformed or Calvinistic Doctrine of the Holy Eucharist* (1846; repr., Eugene, OR: Wipf & Stock, 2000); John Williamson Nevin, "The Doctrine of the Reformed Church on the Lord's Supper," *Mercersburg Review* 2 (1850): 421–548. See also a critical reply to Charles Hodge's review of *The Mystical Presence* and William Cunningham's criticisms of Calvin: John Adger, "Calvin Defended against Drs. Cunningham and Hodge," available at http://www.pcahistory.org/HCLibrary/periodicals/spr/v27/27-1-6.pdf.

149. Nevin, *Mystical Presence*, 155–74.

is a communion with the person of the risen and ascended Christ. It is far more than a legal or a moral union.

Nevin was strongly influenced by the romanticism that dominated philosophical circles from 1760 to 1830 and affected theology for a while after. He was also impacted by Georg Hegel, with his strongly evolutionary and developmental aspects, having edited the second edition of an important Hegelian anthropology in English.[150] This concatenation of inputs also influenced some of his contemporaries, such as John Henry Newman and Charles Darwin. This may account for Nevin's focus on the mystical elements of union with Christ at the expense of the atonement, justification, and election. There is a strongly universalizing tendency in his incarnational theology.[151] His focus was on the participatory rather than the forensic. William Evans points to his failure to integrate these two elements into his understanding of union with Christ. Nevertheless, he was closer to Calvin and the Westminster Assembly on the Lord's Supper than many of his contemporaries in American Presbyterianism.[152]

But Nevin was not alone in bifurcating the imputational and the impartational. In a similar manner, Scottish Common Sense Realism affected Robert L. Dabney, William Cunningham, and Charles Hodge and led to their bewilderment at, and distaste of, Calvin's sacramental theology. For them, theology must be amenable to reason. Throughout his *Systematic Theology*, Hodge buttresses his statements by repeated recourse to common sense. It is hard to avoid the conclusion that these figures viewed with grave suspicion any stress on those aspects of theology that transcended the capacity of the human mind. Nevin's open espousal of a mystical, transcendent strain, less interested in clear doctrinal pronouncements, was met by a rationalism that eschewed anything that smacked of the mysterious. For Hodge and his friends, the focus was on the forensic, on justification and the atonement. The gospel and its entailments were to be clear and comprehensible.[153] An unfortunate split had occurred in Reformed thought. In part, it explains how the doctrine of union with Christ suffered eclipse.

---

150. D. G. Hart, *John Williamson Nevin: High-Church Calvinist* (Phillipsburg, NJ: P&R Publishing, 2005), 76.

151. Evans, *Imputation and Impartation*, 141–83.

152. See William B. Evans, "Twin Sons of Different Mothers: The Remarkable Theological Convergence of John W. Nevin and Thomas F. Torrance," *Haddington House Journal* 11 (2009): 155–73.

153. Evans, *Imputation and Impartation*, 187–227.

Ten Theses on Union with Christ and Transformation

(1) *The union we enjoy with Christ is more real and more fundamental than the union we have with members of our own bodies.* In the words of Nicolaus Cabasilas (1322–?), union with Christ "is closer than any other union which man can possibly imagine and does not lend itself to any exact comparisons." This is why, he says, Scripture does not confine itself to one illustration but provides a wide range of examples: a house and its occupants, wedlock, limbs and the head. Indeed, it is not possible to form an accurate picture even if we take all these metaphors together. For example, the limbs of Christ are joined more firmly to him than to their own bodies, for the martyrs laid down their heads and limbs with exultation and could not be separated from Christ even so far as to be out of earshot of his voice. In short, this union is closer than what joins a man to himself.[154] Again, the children of God are closer to Christ than to their own parents. Separated from our parents, we survive; separated from Christ, we would die.[155] Cabasilas urges constant meditation on Christ as a result of this, and has an extended series of meditations on the Beatitudes from a Christological perspective.[156]

(2) *This is not a union of essence—we do not cease to be human and become God or get merged into God like ingredients in an ontological soup. This is not apotheōsis.* We noted that the Eastern doctrine of deification has at its root a determined preservation of the distinction between Creator and creature. It opposed any suggestion that we partake of the divine essence, since we have to do with the energies of God. Calvin—and Polanus, too—may have overstepped in talking of a union of substance. Yet Calvin's intention was correct; he wanted to stress the reality, extent, and far-reaching effect of this union, which immeasurably exceeds the merely symbolic. Even if we were to suppose it to be purely symbolic, the symbols symbolize something, and it is this something with which we are concerned.

(3) *We do not lose our personal individual identities in some universal, generic humanity.* There is no universal, generic humanity into which we get

---

154. Cabasilas, *Life in Christ*, 5–6.
155. Ibid., 48–49.
156. Ibid., 93–105.

lost as mere broken eggs in some huge ontological omelette. In the indivisible union of three persons in the one being of God, the eternal distinction of each person is maintained. The union of the Son of God with the humanity taken in the incarnation preserves the reality and integrity of the assumed humanity. Christ's union with the church maintains the humanity of the church. The Holy Spirit's indwelling enhances rather than diminishes our humanity. So, too, with our union with Christ: we remain who we are; indeed, we become what God has intended we should be.

(4) *Union with Christ comes to expression in, and is cultivated by, the Word and sacraments.* It is clear that the Holy Spirit unites us to Christ through the instrumentality of the preaching of the Word of God. Both Peter and James attribute the regeneration of believers to the instrumentality of the Word. Peter states that we have been begotten again not by corruptible seed but by the living and abiding Word of God (1 Peter 1:23), while James considers that God in accordance with his own will has brought us forth by the Word of truth to be a kind of firstfruits of his creatures (James 1:18). Both echo the insistence of Paul that his fellow countrymen will be brought to faith through the preaching of Christ. Faith comes through hearing and hearing through the Word of Christ (Rom. 10:9–17). The preaching of the gospel is, so to speak, the midwife by which the Holy Spirit regenerates us and unites us to Christ. While the god of this world has blinded the minds of unbelievers, the God who created the world shines in our hearts to give the light of salvation by his Son, and this he does as "we preach Jesus Christ as Lord" (2 Cor. 4:4–6).[157] Those who hear the voice of the Son of God are called out of death to life, akin to a resurrection or new creation, and so raised with Christ to new and indissoluble life (John 5:24ff.).

John 6 portrays the reality of union with Christ in a sacramental context. Those who eat Christ's flesh and drink his blood have eternal life. This is done by the Holy Spirit (John 6:63). Jesus is not teaching cannibalism, although he uses language that implies cannibalism and caused such offense that large numbers left him, including many of his disciples. The true meaning of this passage is likely to cause great offense. It teaches the extent and closeness of the union that Christ has with his people. Even Baptists who

---

157. See also John 5:24–25; 1 Cor. 1:18–2:5.

do not accept a sacramental interpretation of the chapter agree that it finds its truest fulfillment in the Lord's Supper.[158]

Robert Bruce argued that there is nothing in the Lord's Supper not available in the Word (the sacrament depends on the Word to be a sacrament) but that in the Lord's Supper we "get Christ better."[159] As Augustine described it, it is "a kind of visible word of God."[160] It is the point of union covenantally and personally between Christ and his people.

(5) *The body and blood of Christ are not materially, corporeally, or physically present in the Lord's Supper.* This was the mistake of the Roman Catholic Church, the Lutherans never entirely escaping it. Christ is at the right hand of the Father, qua his humanity, and so he is in one place. Union with Christ is not corporeal but spiritual, effected by the Holy Spirit. As WCF 29.7 puts it, the union we enjoy is real and true, but spiritual.

As surely as we eat the bread and drink the wine, so Christ enters our souls.[161] As WCF 29.7 says, the faithful receive and feed on Christ in the Lord's Supper really and truly. No amount of stress on the spiritual aspect of the Supper, which is of course a correct stress, can ever diminish the real and true feeding that takes place there. As Jesus said, "my flesh is true meat and my blood is true drink" (John 6:51–58). Or in the words of Paul, in union with Christ we are given "one Spirit to drink" (1 Cor. 12:13). As Bernard of Clairvaux penned in his hymn "Jesus, Thou Joy of Loving Hearts" (c. 1150):

We taste thee, O thou living bread, and long to feast upon thee still;
We drink of thee, the fountainhead, and thirst our souls from thee to fill.

158. George R. Beasley-Murray, *John*, Word Biblical Commentary (Waco, TX: Word, 1987), 94–95; D. A. Carson, *The Gospel according to St John* (Leicester, UK: Inter-Varsity Press, 1991), 288–98.

159. Robert Bruce, *The Mystery of the Lord's Supper: Sermons on the Sacrament Preached in the Kirk of Edinburgh in A.D. 1589*, ed. Thomas F. Torrance (London: James Clarke, 1958), 85.

160. Philip Schaff, *Augustin: Letters or Tractates on the Gospel according to St. John*, Nicene and Post-Nicene Fathers of the Christian Church, 1st ser. (Peabody, MA: Hendrickson, 1995), 7:344; *PL*, 35:1840.

161. In the words of Robert Bruce, "I call them signs because they have the Body and Blood of Christ conjoined with them. Indeed, so truly is the Body of Christ conjoined with the bread, and the Blood of Christ conjoined with the wine, that as soon as you receive the bread in your mouth (if you are a faithful man or woman) you receive the Body of Christ in your soul, and that by faith. And as soon as you receive the wine in your mouth, you receive the Blood of Christ in your soul, and that by faith. It is chiefly because of this function that they are instruments to deliver and exhibit the things that they signify . . . [for] the Sacrament exhibits and delivers the thing that it signifies to the soul and heart, as soon as the sign is delivered to the mouth." Bruce, *The Mystery of the Lord's Supper*, 44.

(6) *In the Lord's Supper we are lifted up by the Holy Spirit to feed on Christ.* This is real and true, for it is communion with the Son in the Holy Spirit and thus entails personal access to the Father. We are given to share in the life of the Trinity. In the Supper, the Spirit lifts us up to feed on Christ. Since he is God, he joins things separated by distance, as Calvin said,[162] uniting those that are spatially far apart. The Spirit and the Son are indivisible with the Father in the unity of the Holy Trinity. Moreover, the Spirit's distinctive work is to glorify Christ and lead his people to him through the faith he gives them. Indeed, Paul regards the Spirit as so close to the risen Christ that he can call him "the Spirit of the Lord" and "the Lord, the Spirit" (2 Cor. 3:17).

(7) *We are not hypostatically united to the Son.* There is only one such union—the incarnate Christ, who remains one person forever and ever. The indwelling of the Trinity through the Holy Spirit (e.g., John 14:23) is different. Whereas in the incarnation the Son has indissolubly united himself to a human nature in one person, the Spirit indwells countless human persons. What he does is to enhance our humanity to be what God eternally intended it to be. In this, Jesus Christ is the archetype and exemplar. As man, he was led by the Holy Spirit at all times. He is the Author, Pioneer, and Perfecter of our salvation in his incarnate life and work, sharing our faith, our very nature of flesh and blood, our temptations, our sufferings, our death and burial (Heb. 2:5–18), besides our resurrection (Rom. 8:10–11; 1 Cor. 15:35–50) and ascension.

(8) *We are united with Christ's person.* This goes beyond the indwelling of the Holy Spirit in the church and its members, as explained by Jesus in John 14 and developed by Paul in Romans 8 and Galatians 4. It is grounded in his incarnation—he is forever man and so one with us according to his human nature. In this case, the Holy Spirit unites us to him in a spiritual union. In this union, we all retain our distinctive identities.

The result is that we have more than fellowship with Christ. Fellowship takes place between separate persons by means of presence, recognition, conversation, shared interests, and the like. Adam had fellowship with God before the fall. Redemption has not restored us to the condition of Adam. The incarnation has happened; the Son of God is forever human. The out-

---

162. *Institutes,* 4.17.10.

pouring and indwelling of the Spirit has occurred and endures; the Spirit of God has taken up permanent residence in and with those who love Christ, and in so doing the Holy Trinity now lives in us. It goes beyond communion. It entails union.

It is more than participation in the energies of Christ, contrary to what Michael Horton seems to me to suggest.[163] Horton considers that we have union with God in his workings or makings. He rightly wants to steer clear of the idea that we are united with Christ's essence. This is similar to the cautious approach of Gregory of Nyssa, who was prepared to speak only of participation in the divine energies and rarely mentioned *theōsis*.[164] But the question we posed earlier concerning the incarnate humanity of Christ needs to be addressed. Was the assumed humanity merely taken into union by the energies of God? Was it not the *person* of the Son who united humanity to himself?[165] The human nature of Christ was not simply united to some of God's attributes; if that were so, we would be left with an extreme form of Nestorianism and would have jettisoned the simplicity of God. This union cannot be restricted to union with righteousness, goodness, holiness, or truth, with abstract qualities. Nor is our union only a union with the benefits of Christ, as if we were united with the doctrine of sanctification. It is union with *Christ*.[166]

Since the assumed humanity of Christ participates in the eternal Son, is sanctified and glorified in him, and since we feed on the flesh and blood of Christ, we, too, in Christ are being transformed into his glorious likeness.

(9) *It is effected and developed by the Holy Spirit through faith*, in and through the means of grace: the ministry of the Word, the sacraments, and prayer (WSC 88). It is churchly, not individualistic. It is not a private experience to be developed in isolation. It occurs in the humdrum everyday experience of the means God has appointed, not the superficially exciting or dramatic experiences concocted by human ingenuity.

It is not automatic; it is through faith. There is a certain responsibility on our part to cultivate our union with Christ. Participation in the means of grace is essential, for it is there that God has undertaken to meet with us,

---

163. Horton, *Covenant and Salvation*, 285, 302.
164. Russell, *Deification*, 225–32.
165. Horton, *Covenant and Salvation*, 272–307.
166. I am sure that this is something with which Horton would agree. It is to the apparent drift of his argument that I refer.

and we know that he keeps his appointments.[167] At the same time, it is not an immanent process under our control; it is initiated and developed by the Holy Spirit. It is supernatural; it transcends our capacity to explain. But we can *expect* the Spirit to work with and through the means he himself has appointed for that purpose.

(10) *It will eventually lead to our being "like [Christ]"* (1 John 3:1–2; see also Rom. 8:29–30; 2 Cor. 3:18), for "it is the intention of the gospel to make us sooner or later like God" (Calvin). For the present we are "partakers of the divine nature," having escaped the corruption that is in the world by lust (2 Peter 1:4). When Christ appears at his parousia, however, we will see him as he is, in his glorified humanity, and we will be finally and climactically transformed to be like him, our present lowly bodies changed to be like his glorious body (Phil. 3:20–21). Christ, as Calvin put it, "makes us, ingrafted into his body, participants not only in all his benefits but also in himself," so that "he grows more and more into one body with us, until he becomes completely one with us."[168]

---

167. It was at Passover that the Lamb of God offered himself as the definitive sacrifice for sin; it was when the day of Pentecost had fully come that the Holy Spirit was sent.

168. *Institutes*, 3.2.24.

Union with Christ in Death and Resurrection

Ultimately, our union with Christ will be brought to its fulfillment in the future, at Christ's return, when we will be raised from the dead and our transformation into his image will be complete. In short, union with Christ is to be understood in eschatological terms. It is union with Christ in his death, burial, resurrection, and ascension. As Lane Tipton says, "all saving benefits of the gospel . . . are given to believers only in terms of faith—union with the crucified and resurrected Christ of Scripture."[1]

Union with Christ in His Sufferings

Paul expresses the wish to be conformed to Christ in the likeness of his death, sharing the fellowship of his sufferings (Phil. 3:10):

> that I may know him and the power of his resurrection, and may share his sufferings, becoming like him in his death. (ESV)

When he wrote this, Paul knew from experience what he was describing. He was languishing in a Roman prison, awaiting trial, with the possibility of execution. He did not expect to be sentenced to death; rather, he anticipated fruitful future ministry. In fact, he was eventually released and enjoyed an

---

1. Lane G. Tipton, "Union with Christ and Justification," in *Justified in Christ: God's Plan for Us in Justification*, ed. K. Scott Oliphint (Fearn, Ross-shire, UK: Mentor, 2007), 24–25.

extended period of further apostolic service before his final imprisonment, trial, and execution. Yet Paul could not have known of these future events at the time, and so his condition when he wrote these words was grim. Roman prisons were not the most appealing of places. Paul knew that, throughout his ministry, Jesus had suffered. He faced the militant and potentially murderous opposition of the religious establishment. His disciples often proved feckless and unreliable; they frequently failed to understand what he was saying. He was confronted by sinners, by the onslaughts of the devil and the activities of demons, and by the sheer exhaustion of his constant labors. He was living in a fallen world. Paul, in union with Christ, in measure shared these sufferings. He lists a whole range of them in 2 Corinthians 11:12–33.

> Five times I received at the hands of the Jews the forty lashes less one. Three times I was beaten with rods. Once I was stoned. Three times I was shipwrecked; a night and a day I was adrift at sea; on frequent journeys, in danger from rivers, danger from robbers, danger from my own people, danger from Gentiles, danger in the city, danger in the wilderness, danger at sea, danger from false brothers; in toil and hardship, through many a sleepless night, in hunger and thirst, often without food, in cold and exposure. And, apart from other things, there is the daily pressure on me of my anxiety for all the churches. Who is weak, and I am not weak? Who is made to fall, and I am not indignant? (vv. 24–29 ESV)

These factors are, in some measure, common to all who are united to Christ. He suffered because of who he is; we suffer because we are one with him. We are called to this (Phil. 1:29). There is the suffering that goes with being human in a fallen world: the decay of the body, the sickness that attends it, the process of dying, and death itself. We face bereavement, as loved ones die, whether of old age or suddenly in the prime of life. Tragedy, grief, frustration, disappointment, betrayal by those we trusted, abuse from bullies, slander from the ignorant, irrational opposition from people in power, the shock and demoralization of unemployment, vicious actions by those who take advantage of us—these and many more are the common lot of the human race in a world living in active disobedience to, and defiance of, God its Creator.

Over and above that, Christian believers in general, and ministers of the gospel in particular, face a further set of sufferings that identify us with Christ in his godly anguish and dereliction. There is opposition to our ministries, sometimes with genuine reason but often from irrational self-centeredness and ignorant unbelief. We face the rejection of the gospel and, sometimes worse, complete indifference to it. We are bombarded by temptations of various kinds, and frequently this may meet with a positive response from "the remnants of corruption" within. The world, the flesh, and the devil seem to conspire against us too often. Some may face imprisonment for their faithfulness to Christ. Many each year are martyred. In western Europe the price of faithfulness to the gospel may turn out to be imprisonment or punitive financial penalties as the church resists the demand of godless governments to require practicing homosexuals to receive communion and be appointed to positions of church leadership.

Paul says much the same in 2 Corinthians 4:8–12, in relation to Christian ministry:

> We are afflicted in every way, . . . perplexed, . . . persecuted, . . . struck down, . . . always carrying in the body the death of Jesus. . . . We who live are always being given over to death for Jesus' sake . . . Death is at work in us. (ESV)

In all these passages Paul also highlights compensating features. Just as we are to share in the death of Jesus in practical ways here and now, so we will share in his resurrection. Indeed, in part this is evident even as we suffer. While we are afflicted, we are not crushed; we are not driven to despair; we are not forsaken; we are not destroyed; for the life of Jesus is manifest (now) in our bodies (2 Cor. 4:7–12). In Romans, Paul declares the sufferings of the present time to be insignificant in comparison with the future glory (Rom. 8:18). Later in the chapter in 2 Corinthians he writes of "this slight momentary affliction," stressing its lightness and its transitoriness in contrast to the "eternal weight of glory" that is beyond compare (2 Cor. 4:17). In Philippians his desire to share the sufferings of Christ is so that he might also know "the power of his resurrection" (Phil. 3:10). In short, there are dangers in focusing too much on the glories that await us, if that leads us to discount the reality of present sufferings. If we share the glory of Christ, if we are being transformed from one degree of glory to another, being made partakers of the divine nature, then there is no detour around the equally pertinent reality that we will share the sufferings of Christ. No road to glory avoids the cross. "If we died with him, we will also live with him; if we endure, we will also reign with him" (2 Tim. 2:11–12). Those who reign with Christ are those beheaded for the testimony of Jesus (Rev. 20:4).[2]

Union with Christ in Death and Burial

Here the locus classicus is Paul's words of encouragement in 1 Thessalonians 4:13–17:

> But we do not want you to be uninformed, brothers, about those who are asleep, that you may not grieve as others do who have no hope. For since we believe that Jesus died and rose again, even so, through Jesus, God will bring with him those who have fallen asleep. For this we declare to you by a word from the Lord, that we who are alive, who are left until the coming of the Lord, will not precede those who have fallen asleep. For the Lord himself will descend from heaven with a cry of command, with the voice of an archangel, and with the sound of the trumpet of God. And the dead in Christ will rise first. Then we who are alive, who are left, will be caught up together with them in the clouds to meet the Lord in the air, and so we will always be with the Lord. (ESV)

Paul recognizes that it is natural to mourn the loss of loved ones. Death is an alien intrusion into God's creation, the result of human sin. It is a cruel dissolution of the human being, often preceded by a grim process of decay or a terrible accident. Death is an unknown; we have never experienced it and do not know exactly what lies in store for us. It hangs over us like a threat. In that perspective, mourning is not a sign of a lack of faith; it demonstrates our humanity. Jesus wept at the grave of Lazarus, and bristled with anger at the fact of death and all it entailed. Jesus was sinless and exercised perfect faith. It was because he was human that he wept then and was overcome with grief in Gethsemane later (Luke 22:39–46; John 11:33–38; Heb. 5:7–10).

But Christians are not to mourn like the rest of the world, who have no hope. Their mourning is to be distinctly different. For the unbelieving world, the outlook is hopeless. It can be evaded only by placing a taboo over the subject of death, or by treating it in a flippant and lighthearted manner

---

2. This is a difficult passage to interpret. I am referring to the souls who reign with Christ on the basis that "the first resurrection" (v. 5) is the resurrection of Christ (I know of no other resurrection that could be called the first), and so those who reign with him are united to him in his resurrection, including believers struggling against persecution in the seven churches of Asia Minor, to which Revelation is addressed.

inappropriate to its grim reality. The former modus operandi was typical of the twentieth century. The latter seems the preferred option of more recent times, funeral services being filled with pop songs and expressions of hope that the deceased is looking down on the survivors.

In contrast, Christian mourning is marked by hope. Hope for Paul is not wishful thinking. I hope the soccer team I support, Tottenham Hotspur, will win their next ten games at least. They may do so, but on the other hand, they may lose at least one of them. Hope for Paul is not like that. It relates not to uncertainty but to futurity. We expect God's promises to be brought to complete realization—but at some time in the future. We await the fulfillment; we look for the resurrection of the dead and the life of the world to come. So Christians mourn, but they do so with joyful anticipation for the ultimate consummation of salvation in Jesus Christ.

There are good reasons why this is so. Paul provides them in this passage. The first is that "we believe that Jesus died" (1 Thess. 4:14). *Who* is Jesus? He is the eternal Son of God. He, the Son of God, submitted himself to death, the atoning death of the cross. God himself, the Son of God, has experienced death according to his humanity. From within our own nature, he has shared the experience that we will undergo. He knows exactly what it is like. This is stupendous. We need to consider it, meditating upon it at length. Jesus, the Son of God, has himself gone on the path from death through the tunnel of burial. Human death is an experience now known to God himself.

Second, "we believe that Jesus died *and rose again*" (v. 14). Death was not the end. He conquered it. The Father raised him from the dead by the Holy Spirit (Rom. 8:10–11). There is *a past triumph*. This is why we can grieve with hope, knowing that Christ has experienced death to its fullest and has triumphed over it, rising from the dead on the third day.

We also have confident expectation in the midst of mourning because there is *a present protection*. One of the greatest affirmations in the whole of Scripture is found here. Paul describes believers who have died as "dead in Christ" (1 Thess. 4:16). Union with Christ in his burial is the most triumphant affirmation imaginable. Whatever the process leading up to it, however sad or horrifying the ordeal, once we have died the forces of sin and the decay resulting from it are over. In the words of the hymn "The Strife Is O'er, the Battle Done": "Death's mightiest powers have done their worst" and are now a spent force. Our bodies are lowered into the ground, there to putrefy, rot, and disintegrate. But as these foul forces take their toll on our once-animated features, now reduced to a lifeless corpse engulfed in a disgusting stench, Paul can say that we are "dead *in Christ*." The worst efforts of sin, Satan, and all the concomitants of death can do nothing whatsoever to alter this truth. Our union with Christ is indestructible. No cosmic power can touch us. We are safe in union with the One who is the eternal Son of God.

Moreover, at the parousia the dead in Christ will be at no disadvantage compared to those who are still alive, since the dead will rise first and Christ will bring them *with him*. The implication is that, while in the state of death, they will be *with Christ*. Paul affirms this elsewhere: torn between a desire to die and a wish to remain to serve the church, Paul considers that if he were to die it would be "very far better" (Phil. 1:21). The reason is that even though he would be absent from the body, he would take up residence with the Lord (2 Cor. 5:6–8). This is the language of emigration. As one leaves one's own country and goes to live in a strange land, so we will leave the natural embodied state for the strange land of the intermediate time, but we will simultaneously be domiciled with Christ himself. What safer place could there be?

This is not the main desire of Paul, for his anticipation of the resurrection body surpasses it. In 2 Corinthians 5:1–5, the verbs he uses for our permanent, heavenly body, which we will receive at the resurrection, are all powerful and emotive ones, whereas he is more reticent when it comes to the intermediate state mentioned in verses 6–8. But the point is that our experience of death, burial, and the intermediate state will be in union with Christ. He has gone there before us. We will go there in him.

Union with Christ in Resurrection and Ascension

Tipton correctly affirms that "there is no notion of redemptive life apart from the more basic category of resurrection life, and this resurrection life is given in terms of union with Christ."[3] For this, we need to examine the major treatment Paul gives to the resurrection in 1 Corinthians 15. He starts by describing the core of his gospel, "that Christ died for our sins in accordance with the Scriptures, that he was buried, [and] that he was raised on the third day in accordance with the Scriptures" (vv. 3–4 ESV). Christ's death and resurrection are of first importance, and it is in union with him in his death and resurrection that all the blessings of salvation are given

---

3. Tipton, "Union," 26.

to us. Hence, the great reality of justification is subsumed under the death and resurrection of Christ, for it is in union with him that we are justified through faith. The same applies to adoption, sanctification, and all the other elements of the order of salvation.

Undergirding this is the fact that Christ's resurrection and ours are one reality. In verses 12–19, Paul argues backward and forward from one to the other. If the dead are not raised, then Christ has not been raised. Conversely, if Christ was not resurrected, neither will there be a general resurrection in the future. Moreover, the entire gospel will collapse, and we will have a prospect most bleak. Preaching Christ will be a monumental waste of time, if that is so. In short, the resurrection of Christ and our resurrection stand or fall together.

In contrast to the hypothesis of futility, the reality is glorious. Christ has been raised from the dead (v. 20). Paul could point to a superfluity of witnesses. The Law requires two or three witnesses to establish a thing; with Christ's resurrection there was an overflowing abundance. Paul lists some of these witnesses in verses 8–11, hundreds of whom were still alive when he wrote. Moreover, Christ is the firstfruits of our resurrection. This means not only that his resurrection is first in time, ours following in the future, but that the two are of the same kind. The firstfruits of the harvest are of the same nature as the whole. The first apples are of the same type as the rest that follow; so Christ's resurrection is of the same nature as ours will be. His has already happened, in A.D. 30. Ours will occur at his coming (v. 23), before which he will have subjected all his enemies, in fulfillment of Psalm 110.

Indeed, when we inquire about the nature of the resurrection body, the identity between Christ's resurrection and ours becomes even clearer. There was, of course, an ongoing continuity between Christ's human body before his death and after his resurrection. He was identifiably the same person before and after and even bore the marks of his crucifixion. He ate food, he conversed with his disciples, he broke bread (Luke 24:30, 41–43, etc.). Yet there was also a difference. He was transformed, passing through locked doors (Luke 24:36; John 20:19, 26). Although Christ was not present when Thomas refused to believe the disciples' account of his appearance, when he returned eight days later he knew exactly what Thomas had said (John 20:19–29). He ascended to the Father (Luke 24:50–52; Acts 1:6–11). Afterwards, appearing to the apostles Paul and John, he was suffused in such glory that life and strength was sapped from their bodies (Acts 9:1–9;

Rev. 1:10–20). Paul unfolds these contrasts in 1 Corinthians 15:35–49. Christ, at his conception in the womb of Mary, received a natural body, a body "of the earth," descended from Adam as ours is. In the resurrection, we will be conformed to his glorious body (cf. Phil. 3:20–21) as the second or last Adam, "the man from heaven" (1 Cor. 15:49). The pre-resurrection body is marked by perishability, dishonor, weakness, for it is a natural body, made of dust, of the earth. The resurrection body, in contrast, is one that is imperishable, glorious, powerful, from heaven, and described as "spiritual" or under the direction of the Holy Spirit. The one is received from Adam; the other is from the risen Christ (vv. 42–49).

Therefore, our resurrection bodies will be like Christ's resurrection body, since our resurrection and his are effectively the same reality, separated by indefinite time. There is something of a parallel in this to the Einstein-Podorsky-Bell theory. Einstein postulated that the parts of a subatomic particle, such as a prion, separated by infinite space would behave identically. His theory was confirmed empirically by the Bell experiment in 1964. Here the parts of the resurrection, separated by indefinite time, behave identically.

This conclusion is underlined by Paul's statement in Romans 8:11: "[Since] the Spirit of him who raised Jesus from the dead dwells in you, he who raised Christ from the dead will also give life to your mortal bodies through his Spirit who lives in you." First, the Father raised Christ from the dead by the Holy Spirit; Christ's resurrection was brought about by an engagement of the whole Trinity, as in all the other works of God. Second, Paul says that the Father will raise us from the dead in union with Christ by the Holy Spirit. At our resurrection there will be the same engagement of the whole Trinity as there was when Christ himself was resurrected. The two resurrections are identical in theological terms as well as identical in the outcome they produce. This is so since we have been granted to share the same relation to the Father as the Son enjoys, since we are in union with him, and since God treats us exactly like the Son! Third, the same Spirit of the Father who raised the Son from the dead, and will raise us also, actually lives within us now! We currently experience the resurrection life of Christ through the Holy Spirit, whom the Father has sent to indwell and saturate us. In turn, he produces assurance of our risen salvation, since he is the One who will raise us from the dead in the future, as the Author and Giver of life.

At this point the whole universe should stop for half an hour in utter amazement and wonder. What more can we possibly say?

Christ's resurrection, since it is paradigmatic and definitive of ours, being of the same reality, shapes the whole of salvation in union with Christ. In his resurrection, Christ himself was justified, or vindicated, as the second Adam. He had come to take Adam's place, to undo the damage caused by the first Adam and bring us to a goal greater than Adam could have envisaged. Whereas Adam succumbed to temptation and fell into sin, bringing guilt, condemnation, and death to the entire race, Christ—in union with us—rendered perfect obedience to the Father, and freely suffered the penalty of the broken law on our behalf. Again, in union with us, he was publicly vindicated by the Father when he raised him from the dead by the Holy Spirit. As the second Adam, in our place, on our behalf, and in union with us, he was exalted by the Father in his ascension to his right hand. He "was delivered up for our trespasses and raised for our justification" (Rom. 4:25), "manifested in the flesh, vindicated by the Spirit" (1 Tim. 3:16). Because of the union we sustain to Christ, when he was declared to be the Son of God with power at his resurrection—beyond all probation as the second Adam, as Tipton puts it[4]—so also are we justified in Christ only through faith and raised with him to heavenly places.

As another example, the NT connects Christ's resurrection with our regeneration. This is explicit in 1 Peter 1:3, where Peter states, "Blessed be the God and Father of our Lord Jesus Christ! According to his great mercy, he has caused us to be born again to a living hope through the resurrection of Jesus Christ from the dead." Our regeneration is through Christ's resurrection. His resurrection was his entrance into his new life according to the Spirit (1 Cor. 15:42ff.). He was resurrected in union with his people. They, in union to him, will experience the resurrection in its fullness at his return, but even now we are brought from death in sin to a life of righteousness (Eph. 2:1–10). In short, our regeneration is a new creation (2 Cor. 5:17), a resurrection from the dead. As a new creation, we are raised with Christ, ascended with Christ, seated with Christ in the heavenly places, where he is, at the right hand of the Father. And this is merely the beginning. In the coming ages we will enjoy never-ending and perpetually unfolding kindness flowing from the immeasurable riches of the grace of the Father in Christ by the Holy Spirit (Eph. 2:4–7). Union with Christ is realized in its fullness at the resurrection itself, when we will be like Christ (1 John 3:1–2),[5] for "no

4. Ibid., 27–31.
5. Calvin, *Institutes*, 3.6.5.

one has made progress in the school of Christ who does not joyfully await the day of death and final resurrection."[6]

Baptism

Union with Christ in his death and resurrection comes to expression in baptism. Paul can rebut possible anti-antinomian allegations that the gospel encourages sin by pointing to the fact that we have been baptized into Christ's death and raised to newness of life (Rom. 6:1ff.). The grounds for this are that Jesus considered the cross to be his own baptism. When undergoing baptism at the hands of John in the Jordan and facing the Baptizer's reluctance to administer the rite to him, he insisted on going ahead with it, for it was necessary to fulfill all righteousness (Matt. 3:13–15). There is general agreement that Jesus underwent baptism at the hands of John in view of his eventual atoning death on the cross where he fulfilled righteousness. John's baptism was a baptism of repentance. Jesus had no sin of which to repent. He had no personal need to be baptized. His submission to baptism was in a vicarious capacity, on behalf of his people, whom he was to save from their sins (cf. Matt. 1:21). Thus, it had a prospective force, looking forward to the cross. Later, he explicitly identified his coming sufferings with baptism: "I have a baptism to be baptized with, and how great is my distress until it is accomplished!" (Luke 12:50). At the cross there was the unmitigated judgment of God on human sin and the superlative demonstration of God's grace. Baptism exhibits both elements—death as condemnation of sin and life freely given by God.[7]

In our union with Christ we share in his death and resurrection, signed, sealed, and exhibited in baptism (cf. WCF 27.3; 28.1, 6). Paul develops this theme in a number of places. All who have been baptized into Christ have been united with him in his death and resurrection (Rom. 6:3–11). In baptism we were baptized into Christ, and so we put on Christ (Gal. 3:27). This means that we are made part of one body, the church, formed by the Holy Spirit. The Spirit baptized us into the church, which Paul regards as the same thing as being baptized into Christ: "For just as the body is one and has many members, . . . so it is with Christ. For in one Spirit we were all baptized into one body . . . and were all made to drink of one Spirit" (1 Cor. 12:12–13). Baptism comes

6. Ibid., 3.9.5.
7. See the chapter "The One Baptism Common to Christ and His Church," in Thomas F. Torrance, *Theology in Reconciliation* (Grand Rapids: Eerdmans, 1975), 82–105.

first, the Holy Spirit efficaciously uniting us to Christ in and through it, and thereafter we drink the Spirit—a possible reference to the other sacrament, the Lord's Supper. Again Paul returns to the theme of union with Christ in his death and resurrection, and connects it explicitly with baptism in Colossians 2:11f. Before Paul wrote, Peter's gospel proclamation on the day of Pentecost included the call for baptism and connected it to the reception of the Holy Spirit (Acts 2:38). In view of their collective and individual guilt, and the exaltation of Jesus, the call is for repentance and baptism, in view of which will be given the forgiveness of sins and the gift of the Holy Spirit. Repentance is a gift of God; later chapters in Acts make that clear (Acts 11:18). So, too, baptism is not seen as a human work but as a sacrament ordained by Christ in which the grace of the Holy Spirit is given to God's people through faith, effective in God's time. Paul recalls with approval the words of Ananias given to him after his experience on the way to Damascus: "Rise and be baptized and wash away your sins" (Acts 22:16). Peter writes that "baptism . . . saves" (1 Peter 3:21). These are strong words. It should be self-evident that they do not undermine salvation by grace one whit. Baptism is seen as a work of God. The Spirit works with power in and through it, but as always, his work is not to be reduced to some automatic process; there must be an answering faith from our side, which Paul informs us is a gift of God given to his elect. As Tony Lane says, "this may not accord with the view of the majority of Evangelicals today but they should take up their complaint with the apostles."[8] When we reflect on union with Christ, right at the heart of the gospel, we must hold to its earthiness. Creation is not replaced by redemption. The incarnation is its root; the resurrection of the body is fundamental. So also the earthly, material sacraments are God's prescribed vehicles through which he communicates his mercies to us by the Holy Spirit through faith; that means union with Christ.[9]

Union with Christ in the Consummate Kingdom

Throughout Christ's kingdom, "which shall have no end" (Luke 1:33), our union with Christ will continue, in unbroken and unsullied fulfillment.

---

8. Anthony N. S. Lane, *Justification by Faith in Catholic-Protestant Dialogue: An Evangelical Assessment* (London: T&T Clark, 2002), 186.

9. Underlying opposition to a robust doctrine of the sacraments is a form of gnosticism that has infected evangelical Protestantism and has spread to Reformed churches as well. This takes a subtle form, in which spiritual realities are divorced from the material realm. There needs to be a strong reminder that "in the beginning, God created the heavens *and the earth*" (Gen. 1:1).

There will be work to do. Christ has been given all authority in heaven and on earth. God's plan is for the cosmos to be ruled by the second Adam. Originally, the first Adam was given dominion over the earth. He was made *in* the image of God. But he fell short of God's glory by his sin, and so the earth produced thorns and thistles. In God's sovereign and gracious plan, however, he sent his Son to put things right and, in so doing, to elevate the creation to a higher level and a greater realization than Adam could ever have imagined. The point was that Christ, the second Adam, *is* the image of God. "He is the image of the invisible God, the firstborn of all creation," according to Paul (Col. 1:15). He is "the radiance of the glory of God and the express imprint of his nature" (Heb. 1:3). He is the image of God, in whom the light of the gospel is seen and "the light of the knowledge of the glory of God" is to be found (2 Cor. 4:4–6).

Thus, the author of the Letter to the Hebrews states that God's purpose for mankind is fulfilled in Christ. He cites Psalm 8, which reflects poetically on the account of creation in Genesis 1, and says:

> Now it was not to angels that God subjected the coming world, of which we speak. . . . Now in putting everything in subjection to him, he left nothing outside his control. At present, we do not see everything in subjection to him. But we see Jesus, who for a little while was made lower than the angels, so that by the grace of God he might taste death for everyone, because of the suffering of death, crowned with glory and honour. For it was fitting that he, for whom and by whom all things exist, in bringing many sons to glory should make the pioneer of their salvation perfect through suffering. (Heb. 2:5–10, my translation, viewing the author's comment on Psalm 8 as a chiasmus)

At present we do not see man in control of the universe. Because of sin, he has not fulfilled his mandate. But Jesus, in our nature, is at the right hand of the Father, and he will bring us there to share with him in his eternal rule over the creation. In short, we will share with Christ in governing the renewed heavens and earth. Paul could say that we will judge the world and the fallen angels (1 Cor. 6:1–3), being given to share with Christ in his role as the Judge at the last day. It is one of the spiritual blessings in the heavenly places that we have received in Christ that we will be partners with him and in him in his government of "all things" (Eph. 1:3–10). Calvin wrote that "the hope of the glory of God has shone upon us by the Gospel, which testifies that we shall be partakers of the divine nature, for when we shall see God face to face, we shall be like him (II Pet. 1.4; I John 3.2)."[10] In the words of WLC 90:

Q. 90. What shall be done to the righteous at the day of judgment?

A. At the day of judgment, the righteous, being caught up to Christ in the clouds, shall be set on his right hand, and there openly acknowledged and acquitted, shall join with him in the judging of reprobate angels and men, and shall be received into heaven, where they shall be fully and forever freed from all sin and misery; filled with inconceivable joys, made perfectly holy and happy both in body and soul, in the company of innumerable saints and holy angels, but especially in the immediate vision and fruition of God the Father, of our Lord Jesus Christ, and of the Holy Spirit, to all eternity. And this is the perfect and full communion, which the members of the invisible church shall enjoy with Christ in glory, at the resurrection and day of judgment.

This is more than an academic question. It is greater than life and death. How tragic if, after reading this, you—the reader—are *not* united to Christ. If this is so, the outlook, in the face of death, is—as Paul says—hopeless (1 Thess. 4:13). If you are not united to Christ and all we have said is a purely academic exercise, please consider your situation, believe in Christ, and serve him with all that is in you by the help of the Holy Spirit. Scholarship, theological discussion, bibliographical information is important—but it is far from ultimate. There is something far greater.

If we are united to Christ, endless vistas open . . .

---

10. John Calvin, *Calvin's Commentaries: The Epistles of Paul the Apostle to the Romans and to the Thessalonians*, trans. Ross MacKenzie (Grand Rapids: Eerdmans, 1973), 105.

Bibliography

Adger, John. "Calvin Defended against Drs. Cunningham and Hodge." Available at http://www.pcahistory.org/HCLibrary/periodicals/spr/v27/27-1-6.pdf.

Aquinas, Thomas. *Summa Theologica*.

Athanasius. *Letters to Serapion on the Holy Spirit*.

———. *On the Incarnation*.

———. *Orations against the Arians*.

Ball, John. *A Treatise of the Covenant of Grace*. London: Simeon Ash, 1645.

Barth, Karl. *Church Dogmatics*. Edited by Geoffrey W. Bromiley and Thomas F. Torrance. 14 vols. Edinburgh: T&T Clark, 1956–77.

Bartos, Emil. *Deification in Eastern Orthodox Theology: An Evaluation and Critique of the Theology of Dumitru Staniloae*. Carlisle, UK: Paternoster, 1999.

Bauer, Walter, Frederick William Danker, William Arndt, and F. Wilbur Gingrich, eds. *A Greek-English Lexicon of the New Testament and Other Early Christian Literature*. 3rd ed. Chicago: University of Chicago Press, 2001.

Bavinck, Herman. *In the Beginning: Foundations of Creation Theology*. Edited by John Vriend. Translated by John Bolt. Grand Rapids: Baker, 1999.

———. *Reformed Dogmatics*. Vol. 2, *God and Creation*. Grand Rapids: Baker Academic, 2004.

———. *Reformed Dogmatics*. Vol. 3, *Sin and Salvation in Christ*. Grand Rapids: Baker Academic, 2006.

Beale, G. K. *The Book of Revelation: A Commentary on the Greek Text*. Grand Rapids: Eerdmans, 1999.

Beasley-Murray, George R. *John*. Word Biblical Commentary. Waco, TX: Word, 1987.

Bettenson, Henry, ed. *Documents of the Christian Church*. 2nd ed. London: Oxford University Press, 1963.

Bobrinskoy, Boris. *The Mystery of the Trinity: Trinitarian Experience and Vision in the Biblical and Patristic Tradition*. Translated by Anthony P. Gythiel. Crestwood, NY: St. Vladimir's Seminary Press, 1999.

Bonner, Gerald. "Deification, Divinization." In *Augustine through the Ages: An Encyclopedia*, edited by Allan D. Fitzgerald, OSA, 265–66. Grand Rapids: Eerdmans, 1999.

Braaten, Carl E., and Robert W. Jenson, eds. *Union with Christ: The New Finnish Interpretation of Luther*. Grand Rapids: Eerdmans, 1998.

Bray, Gerald L. *The Doctrine of God*. Leicester, UK: Inter-Varsity Press, 1993.

Bruce, Robert. *The Mystery of the Lord's Supper: Sermons on the Sacrament Preached in the Kirk of Edinburgh in A.D. 1589*. Edited by Thomas F. Torrance. London: James Clarke, 1958.

Bullinger, Heinrich. *De Testamento Seu Foedere Dei Unico & Aeterno Brevis Expositio*. Zürich, 1534.

Cabasilas, Nicolaus. *Life in Christ*. Translated by Margaret I. Lisney. London: Janus, 1995.

Calvin, John. *Calvin: Theological Treatises*. Edited by J. K. S. Reid. Philadelphia: Westminster Press, 1954.

————. *Calvin's Commentaries: The Epistle of Paul the Apostle to the Hebrews and the First and Second Epistles of St. Peter*. Translated by W. B. Johnston. Grand Rapids: Eerdmans, 1963.

————. *Calvin's Commentaries: The Epistles of Paul the Apostle to the Romans and to the Thessalonians*. Translated by Ross MacKenzie. Grand Rapids: Eerdmans, 1973.

————. *Calvin's Commentaries: The Epistles of Paul to the Galatians, Ephesians, Philippians and Colossians*. Translated by T. H. L. Parker. Grand Rapids: Eerdmans, 1965.

————. *Calvin's Commentaries: The First Epistle of Paul the Apostle to the Corinthians*. Edited by Thomas F. Torrance and David W. Torrance. Translated by John W. Fraser. Grand Rapids: Eerdmans, 1960.

————. *Calvin's Commentaries: The Gospel according to St. John 11–21 and the First Epistle of John*. Translated by T. H. L. Parker. Grand Rapids: Eerdmans, 1959.

————. *Commentarii in Epistolas Canonicas*. Ioannis Calvini Opera Omnia. Genève: Librairie Droz, 2009.

————. *Commentarii in Pauli Epistolas*. Ioannis Calvini Opera Omnia. Genève: Librairie Droz, 1992.

————. *Commentarius in Epistolam Pauli Ad Romanos*. Ioannis Calvini Opera Omnia. Genève: Librairie Droz, 1999.

————. *In Evangelium Secundum Johannem Commentarius Pars Altera*. Ioannis Calvini Opera Omnia. Genève: Librairie Droz, 1998.

————. *Institutes of the Christian Religion*. Edited by Ford Lewis Battles and John T. McNeill. Philadelphia: Westminster Press, 1960.

————. *Joannis Calvini Opera Selecta*. Edited by Petrus Barth and Guilelmus Niesel. 5 vols. Munich: Christoph Kaiser, 1926–54.

———. *Opera quae supersunt omnia.* Edited by Guilielmus Baum, Eduardus Cunitz, and Eduardus Reiss. 59 vols. *Corpus Reformatorum*, vols. 29–87. Brunswick: C. A. Schwetschke and Son, 1863–1900.

———. *Selected Works of John Calvin: Tracts and Letters.* Edited by Henry Beveridge and Jules Bonnet. 7 vols. 1858; repr., Grand Rapids: Baker, 1987.

Carpenter, Craig B. "A Question of Union with Christ? Calvin and Trent on Justification." *WTJ* 64 (2002): 363–86.

Carson, D. A. *The Gospel according to St John.* Leicester, UK: Inter-Varsity Press, 1991.

Certain Learned Divines. *Annotations upon All the Books of the Old and New Testament; Wherein the Text Is Explained, Doubts Resolved, Scriptures Paralleled, and Various Readings Observed.* London: John Legatt and John Raworth, 1645. Wing / 351.01.

Christensen, Michael J., and Jeffery A. Wittung, eds. *Partakers of the Divine Nature: The History and Development of Deification in the Christian Traditions.* Grand Rapids: Baker Academic, 2007.

St. Cyril of Alexandria. *On the Unity of Christ.* Edited by John Anthony McGuckin. Crestwood, NY: St. Vladimir's Seminary Press, 1995.

———. *Dialogue on the Most Holy Trinity.*

———. *Expositio Sive Commentarius in Ioannes Evangelium.*

Daley, Brian. "Leontius of Byzantium: A Critical Edition of His Works, with Prolegomena." D.Phil. diss., Oxford University, 1978.

Davis, Leo Donald. *The First Seven Ecumenical Councils (325–787).* Collegeville, MN: Liturgical Press, 1990.

Davis, Thomas J. *The Clearest Promises of God: The Development of Calvin's Eucharistic Teaching.* New York: AMS Press, 1995.

———. *This Is My Body: The Presence of Christ in Reformation Thought.* Grand Rapids: Baker Academic, 2008.

Dolbeau, François. "Nouveaux Sermons de Saint Augustin Pour la Conversion Des Païens et Des Donatistes." *Revue Des Études Augustiniennes* 39, 1 (1993): 57–108.

Duncan, J. Ligon, III, ed. *The Westminster Confession into the 21st Century: Essays in Rememberance [sic] of the 350th Anniversary of the Westminster Assembly.* Vol. 3. Fearn, Ross-shire, UK: Mentor, 2009.

Evans, William B. *Imputation and Impartation: Union with Christ in American Reformed Theology.* Eugene, OR: Wipf & Stock, 2008.

———. "Twin Sons of Different Mothers: The Remarkable Theological Convergence of John W. Nevin and Thomas F. Torrance." *Haddington House Journal* 11 (2009): 155–73.

Fairbairn, Donald. "Patristic Soteriology: Three Trajectories." *JETS* 50, 2 (June 2007): 297–310.

Ferguson, Sinclair B., David F. Wright, and J. I. Packer, eds. *New Dictionary of Theology*. Leicester, UK: Inter-Varsity Press, 1988.

Fesko, J. V. *Last Things First*. Fearn, Ross-shire, UK: Mentor, 2007.

———. "Sanctification and Union with Christ: A Reformed Perspective." *EQ* 82, 3 (2010): 197–214.

Finlan, Stephen. "Can We Speak of *Theōsis* in Paul?" In *Partakers of the Divine Nature: The History and Development of Deification in the Christian Traditions*, edited by Michael J. Christensen and Jeffery A. Wittung, 68–80. Grand Rapids: Baker Academic, 2007.

Fitzgerald, Allan D., OSA, ed. *Augustine through the Ages: An Encyclopedia*. Grand Rapids: Eerdmans, 1999.

Flavel, John. *The Works of John Flavel*. London: Banner of Truth, 1968.

Frend, W. H. C. *The Rise of the Monophysite Movement*. Cambridge: Cambridge University Press, 1972.

Gaffin, Richard B., Jr. "Biblical Theology and the Westminster Standards." *WTJ* 65 (2003): 165–79.

———. *By Faith, Not by Sight: Paul and the Order of Salvation*. Milton Keynes, UK: Paternoster, 2006.

———. *The Centrality of the Resurrection: A Study in Paul's Soteriology*. Grand Rapids: Baker, 1978.

———. "Justification and Union with Christ." In *A Theological Guide to Calvin's Institutes: Essays and Analysis*, edited by David W. Hall and Peter A. Lillback, 248–69. Phillipsburg, NJ: P&R Publishing, 2008.

———. "Union with Christ: Some Biblical and Theological Reflections." In *Always Reforming: Explorations in Systematic Theology*, edited by Anthony T. B. McGowan, 271–88. Leicester, UK: Apollos / Inter-Varsity Press; Downers Grove, IL: IVP Academic, 2006.

Garcia, Mark A. "Imputation and the Christology of Union with Christ: Calvin, Osiander and the Contemporary Quest for a Reformed Model." *WTJ* 68 (2006): 219–51.

———. *Life in Christ: Union with Christ and Twofold Grace in Calvin's Theology*. Milton Keynes, UK: Paternoster, 2008.

Gerrish, B. A. *Grace and Gratitude: The Eucharistic Theology of John Calvin*. Minneapolis: Fortress Press, 1993.

Goodwin, Thomas. *An Exposition of Ephesians Chapter 1 to 2:10*. N.p.: Sovereign Grace Book Club, 1958.

Green, Lowell C. "Faith, Righteousness, and Justification: New Light on Their Development under Luther and Melanchthon." *SCJ* 4 (1972): 65–86.

Grillmeier, Aloys, S.J. *Christ in Christian Tradition*. Vol. 1, *From the Apostolic Age to Chalcedon (451)*. Translated by John Bowden. 2nd rev. ed. Atlanta: John Knox Press, 1975.

———. *Christ in Christian Tradition*. Vol. 2, *From the Council of Chalcedon (451) to Gregory the Great (590–604)*. Pt. 2, *The Church of Constantinople in the Sixth Century*. Translated by John Cawte. London: Mowbray, 1995.

Robert Grosseteste: On the Six Days of Creation: A Translation of the Hexaëmeron. Translated by C. F. J. Martin. Auctores Britannici Medii Aevi. Oxford: Oxford University Press for the British Academy, 1996.

Hall, David W., and Peter A. Lillback, eds. *A Theological Guide to Calvin's Institutes: Essays and Analysis*. Phillipsburg, NJ: P&R Publishing, 2008.

Hallonstein, Gösta. "*Theōsis* in Recent Research: A Renewal of Interest and a Need for Clarity." In *Partakers of the Divine Nature: The History and Development of Deification in the Christian Traditions*, edited by Michael J. Christensen and Jeffery A. Wittung, 281–93. Grand Rapids: Baker Academic, 2007.

Hardy, Edward Rochie. *Christology of the Later Fathers*. Library of Christian Classics. Philadelphia: Westminster Press, 1954.

Harrison, Verna. "Perichoresis in the Greek Fathers." *St. Vladimir's Theological Quarterly* 35 (1991): 53–65.

Hart, D. G. *John Williamson Nevin: High-Church Calvinist*. Phillipsburg, NJ: P&R Publishing, 2005.

Heppe, Heinrich. *Reformed Dogmatics: Set Out and Illustrated from the Sources*. Translated by Ernst Bizer and G. T. Thomson. Grand Rapids: Baker, 1950.

Horton, Michael S. *Covenant and Salvation: Union with Christ*. Louisville: Westminster John Knox Press, 2007.

Hughes, Philip Edgcumbe. *The True Image: The Origin and Destiny of Man in Christ*. Grand Rapids: Eerdmans, 1989.

Husbands, Mark, and Daniel J. Treier, eds. *Justification: What's at Stake in the Current Debates*. Downers Grove, IL: InterVarsity Press, 2004.

Jeffery, Steve, Michael Ovey, and Andrew Sach. *Pierced for Our Transgressions: Recovering the Glory of Penal Substitution*. Wheaton, IL: Crossway, 2007.

Jenson, Robert W. "Response to Mark Seifrid, Paul Metzger, and Carl Trueman on Finnish Luther Research." *WTJ* 65 (2003): 245–50.

Kelly, J. N. D. *Early Christian Doctrines*. London: Adam & Charles Black, 1968.

Kline, Meredith G. *By Oath Consigned: A Reinterpretation of the Covenantal Signs of Circumcision and Baptism*. Grand Rapids: Eerdmans, 1968.

———. "Covenant Theology under Attack." *New Horizons in the Orthodox Presbyterian Church* 15 (February 1994): 3–5.

Lane, Anthony N. S. *John Calvin: Student of the Church Fathers*. Grand Rapids: Baker, 1999.

——. *Justification by Faith in Catholic-Protestant Dialogue: An Evangelical Assessment.* London: T&T Clark, 2002.

Lee, Yang-Ho. "Calvin on Deification: A Reply to Carl Mosser and Jonathan Slater." *SJT* 63 (2010): 272–84.

Leontius of Jerusalem. *Against Nestorius. PG* 86:1512b.

Letham, Robert. "Amandus Polanus: A Neglected Theologian?" *SCJ* 21 (1990): 463–76.

——. "Baptism in the Writings of the Reformers." *SBET* 7, 2 (Autumn 1989): 21–44.

——. "Calling." In *New Dictionary of Theology*, edited by Sinclair B. Ferguson, David F. Wright, and J. I. Packer, 119–20. Leicester, UK: Inter-Varsity Press, 1988.

——. " 'In the Space of Six Days': The Days of Creation from Origen to the Westminster Assembly." *WTJ* 61 (1999): 149–74.

——. *The Holy Trinity: In Scripture, History, Theology, and Worship.* Phillipsburg, NJ: P&R Publishing, 2004.

——. *The Lord's Supper: Eternal Word in Broken Bread.* Phillipsburg, NJ: P&R Publishing, 2001.

——. "The Man-Woman Debate: Theological Comment." *WTJ* 52 (1990): 65–78.

——. *Through Western Eyes: Eastern Orthodoxy; A Reformed Perspective.* Fearn, Ross-shire, UK: Mentor, 2007.

——. *The Westminster Assembly: Reading Its Theology in Historical Context.* Phillipsburg, NJ: P&R Publishing, 2009.

——. *The Work of Christ.* Leicester, UK: Inter-Varsity Press, 1993.

Liddell, Henry George, and Robert Scott. *A Greek-English Lexicon.* Revised by Henry Stuart Jones. 9th ed. Oxford: Clarendon Press, 1940.

Louth, Andrew. *John Damascene: Tradition and Originality in Byzantine Theology.* Oxford: Oxford University Press, 2002.

Louw, Johannes P., and Eugene A. Nida, eds. *Greek-English Lexicon of the New Testament Based on Semantic Domains.* New York: United Bible Societies, 1988.

Mannermaa, Tuomo. "Justification and *Theōsis* in Lutheran-Orthodox Perspective." In *Union with Christ: The New Finnish Interpretation of Luther*, edited by Carl E. Braaten and Robert W. Jenson, 25–41. Grand Rapids: Eerdmans, 1998.

——. "Why Is Luther So Fascinating? Modern Finnish Luther Research." In *Union with Christ: The New Finnish Interpretation of Luther*, edited by Carl E. Braaten and Robert W. Jenson, 1–20. Grand Rapids: Eerdmans, 1998.

Martin, Hugh. *The Atonement: In Its Relations to the Covenant, the Priesthood, the Intercession of Our Lord.* Edinburgh: Lyon and Gemmell, 1877.

Mathison, Keith A. *Given for You: Reclaiming Calvin's Doctrine of the Lord's Supper.* Phillipsburg, NJ: P&R Publishing, 2002.

McCormack, Bruce L. *For Us and Our Salvation: Incarnation and Atonement in the Reformed Tradition.* Studies in Reformed Theology and History. Princeton: Princeton Theological Seminary, 1993.

————. "What's at Stake in the Current Debates over Justification? The Crisis of Protestantism in the West." In *Justification: What's at Stake in the Current Debates*, edited by Mark Husbands and Daniel J. Treier, 81–117. Downers Grove, IL: InterVarsity Press, 2004.

McGowan, Anthony T. B., ed. *Always Reforming: Explorations in Systematic Theology*. Leicester, UK: Apollos / Inter-Varsity Press; Downers Grove, IL: IVP Academic, 2006.

McGrath, Alister E. *Thomas F. Torrance: An Intellectual Biography*. Edinburgh: T&T Clark, 1999.

McGuckin, John Anthony. *St. Cyril of Alexandria and the Christological Controversy: Its History, Theology, and Texts*. Crestwood, NY: St. Vladimir's Seminary Press, 2004.

McKim, Donald K. *Ramism in William Perkins' Theology*. New York: Peter Lang, 1987.

Metzger, Paul Louis. "Mystical Union with Christ: An Alternative to Blood Transfusions and Legal Fictions." *WTJ* 65 (2003): 201–13.

Meyendorff, John. *Christ in Eastern Christian Thought*. Crestwood, NY: St. Vladimir's Seminary Press, 1975.

Migne, J. P., et al., eds. *Patrologia graeca*. Paris: 1857–66.

————. *Patrologia Latina*. Paris, 1878–90.

Morris, Edward D. *Theology of the Westminster Symbols: A Commentary Historical, Doctrinal, Practical on the Confession of Faith and Catechisms, and the Related Formularies of Presbyterian Churches*. Columbus, OH, 1900.

Morris, Leon. *The Apostolic Preaching of the Cross*. London: Tyndale Press, 1955.

Mosser, Carl. "The Greatest Possible Blessing: Calvin and Deification." *SJT* 55 (2002): 36–57.

Müeller, John Thomas. *Christian Dogmatics*. St. Louis: Concordia, 1934.

Muller, Richard A. *After Calvin: Studies in the Development of a Theological Tradition*. Oxford: Oxford University Press, 2003.

————. *Christ and the Decree: Christology and Predestination in Reformed Theology from Calvin to Perkins*. Grand Rapids: Baker, 1986.

————. *The Unaccommodated Calvin: Studies in the Foundation of a Theological Tradition*. New York: Oxford University Press, 2000.

Murray, John. "Definitive Sanctification." *CTJ* 2, 1 (1967): 5–21.

————. *Redemption Accomplished and Applied*. London: Banner of Truth, 1961.

Nellas, Panayiotis. *Deification in Christ: Orthodox Perspectives on the Nature of the Human Person*, edited by Norman Russell. Crestwood, NY: St. Vladimir's Seminary Press, 1987.

Nevin, John Williamson. "The Doctrine of the Reformed Church on the Lord's Supper." *Mercersburg Review* 2 (1850): 421–548.

———. *The Mystical Presence: A Vindication of the Reformed or Calvinistic Doctrine of the Holy Eucharist*. Eugene, OR: Wipf & Stock, 2000.

Norris, Richard A., Jr. *The Christological Controversy*. Philadelphia: Fortress Press, 1980.

Old, Hughes Oliphant. *The Shaping of the Reformed Baptismal Rite in the Sixteenth Century*. Grand Rapids: Eerdmans, 1992.

Oliphint, K. Scott, ed. *Justified in Christ: God's Plan for Us in Justification*. Fearn, Ross-shire, UK: Mentor, 2007.

Ong, Walter J. *Ramus, Method and the Decay of Dialogue*. Cambridge, MA: Harvard University Press, 1958.

Oxford Dictionary of National Biography. Available at http://www.oxforddnb.com.

Ozment, Steven. *The Age of Reform 1250–1550*. New Haven: Yale University Press, 1980.

Pelikan, Jaroslav. *The Christian Tradition*. Vol. 1, *The Emergence of the Catholic Tradition (100–600)*. Chicago: University of Chicago Press, 1971.

———. *The Christian Tradition*. Vol. 2, *The Spirit of Eastern Christendom*. Chicago: University of Chicago Press, 1974.

Percival, Henry R. *The Seven Ecumenical Councils of the Undivided Church: Their Canons and Dogmatic Decrees*. Select Library of Nicene and Post-Nicene Fathers of the Christian Church, 2nd ser. Edinburgh: T&T Clark, 1997.

Polanus, Amandus. *Partitiones Theologicae*. 2nd ed. Basel, 1590.

———. *Syntagma Theologiae Christianae*. Geneva: Petri Auberti, 1612.

Prestige, G. L. *Fathers and Heretics*. London: SPCK, 1940.

Relton, Herbert M. *A Study in Christology: The Problem of the Relation of the Two Natures in the Person of Christ*. London: SPCK, 1917.

Russell, Norman. *Cyril of Alexandria*. London: Routledge, 2000.

———. *The Doctrine of Deification in the Greek Patristic Tradition*. Oxford: Oxford University Press, 2004.

Schaff, Philip. *Augustin: Letters or Tractates on the Gospel according to St. John*. Nicene and Post-Nicene Fathers of the Christian Church, 1st ser. Peabody, MA: Hendrickson, 1995.

———. *The Creeds of Christendom*. 3 vols. Grand Rapids: Baker, 1966.

Seifrid, Mark A. "Paul, Luther, and Justification in Gal 2:15–21." *WTJ* 65 (2003): 215–30.

Sellers, R. V. *The Council of Chalcedon: A Historical and Doctrinal Survey*. London: SPCK, 1953.

Slater, Jonathan. "Salvation as Participation in the Humanity of the Mediator in Calvin's Institutes of the Christian Religion: A Reply to Carl Mosser." *STJ* 58 (2005): 39–58.

Spear, Wayne. "The Nature of the Lord's Supper according to Calvin and the Westminster Assembly," and "Calvin and Westminster on the Lord's Supper: Exegetical and Theological Considerations." In *The Westminster Confession into the 21st Century: Essays in Rememberance [sic] of the 350th Anniversary of the Westminster Assembly*. Vol. 3, edited by J. Ligon Duncan III, 355–414. Fearn, Ross-shire, UK: Mentor, 2009.

Staniloae, Dumitru. *The Experience of God: Orthodox Dogmatic Theology*. Vol. 1, *Revelation and Knowledge of the Triune God*. Ed. and trans. Ioan Ionita and Robert Barringer. Brookline, MA: Holy Cross Orthodox Press, 1994.

Starr, James. "Does 2 Peter 1:4 Speak of Deification?" In *Partakers of the Divine Nature: The History and Development of Deification in the Christian Traditions*, edited by Michael J. Christensen and Jeffery A. Wittung, 81–92. Grand Rapids: Baker Academic, 2007.

Stedman, Rowland. *The Mystical Union of Believers with Christ, or A Treatise Wherein That Great Mystery and Priviledge of the Saints Union with the Son of God Is Opened*. London: W. R. for Thomas Parkhurst, at the Golden-Bible on London-Bridge, under the gate, 1668. Wing / 335:13.

Stibbs, Allan M. *The Meaning of the Word "Blood" in Scripture*. London: Tyndale Press, 1948.

Suh, Chul Won. *The Creation Mediatorship of Jesus Christ*. Amsterdam: Rodopi, 1982.

Tipton, Lane G. "Union with Christ and Justification." In *Justified in Christ: God's Plan for Us in Justification*, edited by K. Scott Oliphint, 23–50. Fearn, Ross-shire, UK: Mentor, 2007.

Torrance, Thomas F. *Incarnation: The Person and Life of Christ*. Milton Keynes, UK: Paternoster, 2008.

———. *Scottish Theology: From John Knox to John McLeod Campbell*. Edinburgh: T&T Clark, 1996.

———. *Theology in Reconciliation*. Grand Rapids: Eerdmans, 1975.

Trueman, Carl R. "Is the Finnish Line a New Beginning? A Critical Assessment of the Reading of Luther Offered by the Helsinki Circle." *WTJ* 65 (2003): 231–44.

Trumper, Tim J. R. "Covenant Theology and Constructive Calvinism." *WTJ* 64 (2002): 387–404.

Von Rad, Gerhard. *Genesis: A Commentary*. Rev. ed. Philadelphia: Westminster Press, 1961.

Vos, Geerhardus. *The Pauline Eschatology*. Grand Rapids: Eerdmans, 1972.

Wallace, Ronald S. *Calvin's Doctrine of the Word and Sacrament*. Edinburgh: Oliver and Boyd, 1953.

Wallace-Hadrill, D. S. *Christian Antioch: A Study of Early Christian Thought in the East*. Cambridge: Cambridge University Press, 1982.

Ward, Timothy. *Words of Life: Scripture as the Living and Active Word of God*. Downers Grove, IL: IVP Academic, 2009.

Ware, Timothy. *The Orthodox Church*. London: Penguin Books, 1969.

Watson, Francis. *Text, Church, and World: Biblical Interpretation in Theological Perspective*. Edinburgh: T&T Clark, 1994.

Weinandy, Thomas G. "Cyril and the Mystery of the Incarnation." In *The Theology of St. Cyril of Alexandria: A Critical Appreciation*, edited by Thomas G. Weinandy and Daniel A. Keating, 23–54. London: T&T Clark, 2003.

Wenger, Thomas L. "The New Perspective on Calvin: Responding to Recent Calvin Interpretations." *JETS* 50 (2007): 311–28.

Wenham, Gordon J. *Genesis 1–15*. Word Biblical Commentary. Waco, TX: Word, 1987.

Wesche, Kenneth Paul. *On the Person of Christ: The Christology of Emperor Justinian*. Crestwood, NY: St. Vladimir's Seminary Press, 1991.

Williams, A. N. *The Ground of Union: Deification in Aquinas and Palamas*. New York: Oxford University Press, 1999.

Wing, Donald. *Short-Title Catalogue of Books Printed in England, Scotland, Ireland, Wales and British America, and of English Books Printed in Other Countries, 1641–1700*. New York: Index South, 1945.

Zanchius, Hieronymous. *Operum Theologicorum Omnium*. Amsterdam: Stephanus Gamonentus, 1613.

Index of Scripture

Genesis
1—15, 140
1–15—11n5
1:1—11, 12, 139n9
1:1–2—9
1:2—11, 46, 58
1:2–5—9
1:3—10, 11, 12, 13
1:4—10
1:6—10
1:6–8—10
1:7—10
1:9—10
1:9–10—10
1:11–12—10
1:14–15—10
1:14–16—10
1:16—10
1:17—10
1:20–21—10
1:20–30—10
1:21—10
1:24—10
1:25—10
1:26—12
1:26–27—10, 11, 12, 13
1:27—12
1:28–30—15
2—15
2:15–17—57

2:16—15
2:21–22—15
3—16
3:8—15
3:14–19—17
3:22—11
11:7—11
12:1–3—46
17:7–8—36

Exodus
23:6–8—63
34:7—63

Leviticus
4–5—61

Deuteronomy
27:25—63

Joshua
7:1–26—58

Psalms
8—17, 39, 140
8:3–8—15
82—100
110—135
115:4–8—93
146:1—21

Proverbs
17:15—63
17:26—63
18:5—63
24:24—63

Isaiah
5:23—63
6:8—11
42:1—69n28
44:6-8—16

Jeremiah
11:4—36
24:7—36
30:22—36
31:33—36, 45
32:38—36

Ezekiel
36:27—46

Joel
2:28—45

Matthew
1:18—20
1:18-25—20
1:21—138
3:13-15—138
4:1-2—20
4:1-10—60
6:9—54
8:24—20
11:19—20
11:25-27—19
12:18—69n28
20:28—59, 60
26:26-29—60

26:39—58
27:57-66—21

Mark
6:3—20
10:45—59, 60
15:43-47—21

Luke
1:26-38—20
1:33—139
1:34-35—20, 32, 46, 58
1:41-44—46
1:67—46
2:25-28—47
2:40-52—20, 47
2:52—20, 58
3:16—47
3:22—47
4:1—47
4:14—47
4:17—47
11:2—54
12:50—138
22:19—60
22:31-32—38
22:39-46—132
23:50-56—21
24:30—135
24:50-51—39
24:50-52—135

John
1—12
1:1-4—19, 21
1:3—12
1:4—12
1:13—20
1:14-18—19, 21

1:32–33—47

2:1–11—20

3:1–15—73

3:6—69

4:4–7—20

4:34—58

5:16–47—19, 53

5:24—124

5:24–25—124n157

6:37–40—65

6:44–45—51, 73

6:51—61

6:51–58—125

6:63—124

6:64–65—51, 73

7:37–39—48, 103

8:46—58

10:22–36—19, 53

11–21—108n78

11:32–38—20

11:33–38—132

11:50—61

13:18—67, 69

14—126

14–17—48

14:1—19, 48, 53

14:7–11—19, 53

14:7–20—19

14:8–10—48

14:10–11—48

14:16—4, 96

14:16–17—96

14:16–23—48, 103

14:20—4, 49

14:23—4, 49, 94, 97, 126

15:16—69

15:19—69

16:8–11—48, 103

16:8–15—103

16:12–15—48

16:13–14—48

17:4—58

17:21—4, 108

17:21–24—19

17:22–23—5

17:23—54

19:25–27—20

19:38–42—21

20:19—135

20:19–29—135

20:26—135

20:28—19

Acts

1:6–11—135

2—50

2:32–33—48

2:33–36—103

2:38—139

9:1–9—135

11:18—139

13:2—69

22:16—139

Romans

1:19–23—93

3:21—6

3:23—96

3:25—59

3:26—57

4—79

4:25—6, 59, 62, 79, 137

5:8—59, 61

5:12–21—5, 57, 59, 62

5:17—5

6:1—6, 65, 79, 138

6:1–23—87

6:3–4—6

6:3–11—138
6:5—103
8—54, 126
8:3—22
8:10–11—86, 126, 133
8:11—136
8:15–16—88
8:15–17—54
8:18—131
8:29—42
8:29–30—65, 128
8:30—90
10:9–17—124
11:17—42

1 Corinthians
1:18–2:5—124n157
1:30—77, 80
3:9–11—119
6:1–3—140
6:11—69
6:15—105
6:19—99
6:19–20—87
10:16–17—121
11:7—14n13
11:24—60, 105
12:3—69
12:12–13—138
12:13—69, 125
15—6, 134
15:3—61
15:3–4—134
15:8–11—135
15:12–19—6, 135
15:19–23—6
15:20—135
15:20–23—57
15:22—60

15:23—135
15:27—39
15:27–28—114n121
15:35—6
15:35–49—136
15:35–50—126
15:42—137
15:42–49—136
15:45–49—14
15:49—136

2 Corinthians
1:8–11—86
1:21–22—90
3:7–11—97
3:16–17—51
3:17—126
3:17–18—86, 103
3:18—52, 86, 94, 97, 128
4:4—14, 86
4:4–6—124, 140
4:7—131
4:7–12—131
4:7–18—86
4:8–12—131
5:1–5—134
5:6–8—134
5:14–15—61
5:17—88, 137
5:19—21
5:21—61
11:12–33—130
11:24–29—130

Galatians
1:8–9—73
2:20—99
3—22
3:27—43, 138

4—54, 126
4:4—20, 22, 50
4:4-6—50, 54
4:6—51, 88
5:22—87

Ephesians
1—97
1:3—46, 79
1:3-4—4
1:3-5—4
1:3-10—140
1:3-14—4, 78, 85
1:4—65, 66, 67, 72
1:6-7—81
1:7—4
1:10—4, 13, 116n126
1:13-14—4, 90
1:15—85
2:1—5, 51, 73
2:1-7—86
2:1-10—137
2:4-7—137
2:6—60
2:8-9—73
4:4—69
4:15—42
4:24—13, 87
5—106
5:30—105
5:31—106
5:31-32—119
5:32—106

Philippians
1:12-26—86
1:21—134
1:29—130
2:6—22

3:10—129, 131
3:20-21—128, 136

Colossians
1:13—12, 87
1:15—14, 86, 140
1:16-17—12
1:24—86
2:11—139
3:10—13, 87

1 Thessalonians
4:13—141
4:13-17—132
4:14—133
4:16—133

1 Timothy
2:6—61
3:16—137

2 Timothy
1:9—65
2:11-12—131-32

Titus
3:5—103

Hebrews
1:1-4—37
1:1-14—22
1:2—13
1:3—13, 14, 140
2—22
2:5-9—17
2:5-10—140
2:5-18—22, 126
2:8-9—17
2:15-18—20

3:7–4:11—10n3
4:14–16—59
4:14–5:10—21, 22, 62
5:7–10—132
6:18–20—62
7:23–8:1—62
9:11–10:14—62
9:14—49
9:28—61
10:1–14—59
10:7—58

James
1:18—124
3:9—14n13

1 Peter
1:3—137
1:3–4—5
1:5—89
1:20—69n28
1:23—124

2:5—69n28
2:21—59
2:21–24—61
3:18—59, 61
3:21—139

2 Peter
1:3–4—96
1:4—94, 96n33, 106, 117, 118, 128, 140–41

1 John
3:1–2—52, 94, 97, 128, 137
3:2—86, 140–41
3:24—51

Revelation
1:10–20—135–36
20:4—132
20:5—132n2
21:3—36
21:27—66

Index of Subjects and Names

Aaron, 62
Abrahamic covenant, 36, 46
Achan, 58
active obedience of Christ, 57, 59
Adam
    disobedience of, 16–17, 57–58, 81, 137, 140
    in image of God, 13
    as representative of human race, 5–6, 62
adoption, 8, 54, 76, 80, 90
adornment, of world, 9
angels, election of, 72
Apollinarianism, 23
Apollinaris, 23, 26, 34
apotheōsis, 91, 92, 123
Arianism, 23
Arios, 23
Arminianism, 75, 76, 88
Arminius, Jacobus, 70
artificial analogy (Stedman), 119
assurance, 66, 76
Athanasius, 70, 91, 92–94, 107
atonement, 57, 91
    and election, 68
    and incarnation, 41
    justice of, 63
    and justification, 65
    and union with Christ, 60–65
Augsburg Confession, 77
Augustine, 67, 72, 100–101

baptism, 50, 120–21, 138–39
    Calvin on, 103, 111–12

Barth, Karl, 12, 70
Bavinck, Herman, 45, 47, 72
Bernard of Clairvaux, 125
biblical theology, 89
Bobrinskoy, Boris, 46, 47
Bonner, Gerald, 100
Bray, Gerald, 48–49
Bruce, Robert, 125
Bullinger, Heinrich, 114n122

Cabasilas, Nicolaus, 99, 123
Calvin, John, 1, 128, 140
    on deification, 107, 113, 115
    on election, 66
    on energies of God, 123
    on Holy Spirit, 51, 52
    on humanity of Christ, 39–40
    on justification, 74, 77–78
    on sanctification, 77–78
    on union with Christ, 2–3, 32, 42–43,
        103–15
cannibalism, 124
Cappadocians, 34
Christian life, 88–90, 97
Christocentrism, 102
Christology, development of, 23–36
christotokos, 23
church, 127
communicatio idiomatum, 115
communion with Christ, 108–9, 119, 127
conjugal analogy (Stedman), 119
Consensus Tigurinus, 114n122

consummation, 139–41
conversion, 88
corporal analogy (Stedman), 119
corporate solidarity, 58
cosmos, renovation of, 72
Council of Chalcedon (451), 26–29
Council of Constantinople (381), 23
Council of Constantinople (553), 32, 35
Council of Ephesus (431), 25, 29
Council of Nicaea (325), 23
covenants, promise of, 36–37
creation, 9–18
Creator-creature distinction, 15–16, 23, 36,
    91, 99, 101, 123
Cunningham, William, 120, 122
Cyril of Alexandria, 24–25, 26, 27, 28, 30,
    92, 94–95, 107

Dabney, Robert L., 120, 122
Darwin, Charles, 122
Day of Atonement, 62
day of judgment, 141
death, 132–33
decrees of God, 65n13
definitive sanctification, 87
deification, 31–32, 36, 94, 101–2, 123
    in Calvin, 107, 113, 115
Dunn, James D. G., 6n16

Eastern church, 36, 91, 92, 100, 103, 123
Edict of Justinian (551), 33
Edwards, Jonathan, 2
effectual calling, 88
Einstein-Bell-Podosky theory, 7, 136
election, 37, 79
    general and special, 70
    and union with Christ, 65–72
energies of God, 92, 123, 127
enhypostatis, 30, 31
eschatological transformation. See theōsis

Eucharist. See Lord's Supper
Eunomios, 23
Eutyches, 25–28, 34, 91, 95
Evans, William B., 2, 32n45, 52, 122
exile, 46
ex opere operato, 120

faith, 52, 88
    Calvin on, 110
    and justification, 73–74, 75–76
    as living faith, 75
    and union with Christ, 127
fall, 16–18, 130
fellowship, 109, 126
Finlan, Stephen, 97n36
Finnish school of Luther interpretation,
    101–2
firstfruits, 135
Flavel, John, 54–55
Formula of Concord, 77
fruit of the Spirit, 87

Gaffin, Richard B., Jr., 80n59, 89–90
Garcia, Mark, 107
Geneva Catechism, 104
glorification, 80, 89, 90, 91
glory, 96
gnosticism, 139n9
God
    attributes of, 92
    as Father, 53–54
    glory of, 86, 100
    justice of, 71–72
    sovereignty of, 10
Goodwin, Thomas, 71
good works, 74n47
grace, 72, 76, 78
Gregory Nazianzen, 23
Gregory of Nyssa, 92, 127
Gregory Palamas, 92, 101

Grillmeier, Aloys, 30, 34, 35
Grosseteste, Robert, 38

Hallonstein, Gösta, 101
Harnack, Adolf von, 100
Hegel, Georg, 122
Heidegger, John Henry, 80
Hellenistic dualism, 96n33
Heppe, Heinrich, 80
Heshus, Tileman, 112
high priest, 62
history of redemption, 36–37
Hodge, Charles, 2, 122
holiness, 13–14
Holy of Holies, 62
Holy Spirit, 11, 32n45
    and baptism, 138–39
    Calvin on, 108
    and communion with Christ, 112
    as earnest, 90
    and faith, 110
    indwelling of, 47, 49–50, 54, 85, 96, 124,
        127
    in life and ministry of Jesus, 46–47
    at Pentecost, 48–52, 98
    promise of, 45–46
    and sonship, 54
    and union with Christ, 42–43, 51, 52–53,
        114, 118, 128
    and work of Christ, 110
hope, 133
Horton, Michael, 85n2, 127
hypostasis, 30–31, 33
hypostatic union, 28–29, 54, 126

image of Christ, 74, 92, 96
image of God, 10, 11, 13–14, 16, 52, 54, 86
imputation, 6n16, 75, 81
incarnation, 1, 17, 19–43, 35, 54, 93,
        98–100, 108, 116

in Christ, 7, 65, 68–69, 71, 72, 97
individualism, 58
Irish Articles, 77
Israel, election of, 70

Jesus Christ
    ascension of, 42
    baptism of, 47, 98
    birth of, 20, 22
    death of, 86, 133–34
    deity of, 22, 36, 59
    as fulfillment of covenant promises, 36–37
    glorification of, 48
    humanity of, 19–22, 36, 39–40, 58, 59,
        116. See also incarnation
    as image of God, 14, 54, 86, 140
    intercession of, 38
    lordship of, 14, 19
    as Mediator, 67, 68, 71
    as mediator of creation, 12–13, 39
    obedience of, 57–60, 62, 74, 78, 81
    as our representative, 5–6, 57, 61–62, 83
    resurrection of, 85–86, 133, 134–37
    return of, 100, 128, 129, 134, 137
    righteousness of, 80–81
    as second Adam, 14, 18, 64
    as substitute, 59, 60–61
    sufferings of, 129–31
    temptation of, 59
    two natures of, 27
    union with his church, 37–38, 68
    union with our human nature, 37–38
John, on union with Christ, 4–5
John the Baptist, 46–47
    justification, 88, 91, 111
    and faith, 2, 52, 73–74, 102
    as "main hinge", 3
    and sanctification, 2
    and union with Christ, 5–6, 73–81
Justinian I, Emperor, 28, 32–35

Kelly, J. N. D., 25
knowledge, 13–14
Knox, John, 120

Lane, Tony, 7, 42, 52, 77–78, 139
law and grace, 78
legal aspect, to union with Christ, 51–52, 57
Leo, Pope, 26, 29
Leontius of Byzantium, 30–31, 33
Leontius of Jerusalem, 30, 31–32, 33
Logos, 12, 19, 24, 28, 33–35
Lord's Supper, 32, 50, 95, 105, 120–21, 124–25
    Calvin on, 112–13
    Polanus on, 116, 119
Lutherans, 74
    on justification, 82
    on Lord's Supper, 114–15, 120
Luther, Martin, 74, 102

Maastricht, Hendrik van, 80
man, creation of, 13–14, 15–16
Mannermaa, Tuomo, 102
Marcellus of Ancyra, 39n70
Marcian, Emperor, 26
marriage, 98n37
Martin, Hugh, 64–65
Mary, 20, 46
    as theotokos, 23, 24–25, 27
Maximus the Confessor, 95
McCormack, Bruce, 32n45
means of grace, 127
Melanchthon, Philipp, 2
metaphor, 53
metochoi, 94
Meyendorff, John, 31
Monophysites, 28–30, 35
moral union, 52
Morris, Edward, 77
Mosaic covenant, 36, 46, 63
Mosser, Carl, 113

mourning, 132–33
Muller, Richard, 2, 69n27, 115n124
Murray, John, 1, 87n3, 89
mystical elements, of union, 121–22

natural analogy (Stedman), 51–52, 119
nature, 33–34
Nellas, Panayiotis, 99
neoorthodox scholars, 2
Nestorianism, 26, 28–29, 35, 39–40,
    113–14
Nestorius, 23–25
Nevin, John W., 121–22
new covenant, 36, 45
new creation, 46, 58, 86, 137
new life, 121
Newman, John Henry, 18, 21, 122
New Perspective on Paul, 6n16
Niceno-Constantinopolitan creed, 21, 39n70

Ollerton, Andrew, 114n122
order, of creation, 10
ordo salutis, 2, 76, 88–91
Origen, 92, 95
Osiander, 77, 107n75, 114
Ozment, Steven, 102

pantheism, 99
partakers of divine nature, 80, 94, 128, 131,
    141
    Calvin on, 39, 66, 104, 106, 111–12
participation, 94–95. See also theōsis
passive obedience of Christ, 59
Paul
    on Christian life, 97
    on creation, 12–13
    on election, 65
    on humanity of Christ, 21–22
    on image of God, 13–14
    on justification, 5–6, 73

on the resurrection, 6–7
on sanctification, 6
on substitutionary atonement, 61
on suffering, 129–30
on union with Christ, 4
Pentecost, 42, 45–46, 48–52, 96
perichoresis, 48–49
perseverance, 76, 89, 90
Peter
  on divine nature, 96
  at Pentecost, 48
  on substitutionary atonement, 61
  on union with Christ, 5
pneumatocentrism, 103
Polanus, Amandus, 69–71, 72, 79–80,
  115–19, 123
preterition, 71–72
prosōpon, 24, 25, 31
Puritanism, 3

Rad, Gerhard Von, 11
Ramus, Petrus, 70n32
rationalism, 122
Reformed theology, on union with Christ,
  102–23
regeneration, 51, 73–74, 88, 111, 137
Relton, Herbert M., 30
representation, 57–83
resurrection, 6–7, 14, 129, 134–38
resurrection body, 134–36
righteousness, 13–14, 80–81, 111
Roman Catholic Church
  on justification, 74, 75, 80, 82
  on sacraments, 120
romanticism, 122
Russell, Norman, 92–95

sacraments, 120–21, 124–25
  Calvin on, 111–13
  Polanus on, 116

sacrifice, 60–61
sanctification, 2, 6, 73, 74n47, 76, 89–90
  as ethical, 87–88
  as spacial, 87
saving faith, 73
Scots Confession, 77, 120
Scottish Common Sense Realism, 122
second Adam, 14, 18, 26, 58, 59–60, 64, 86,
  137, 140
Second Helvetic Confession, 77
Sellers, R. V., 28, 29, 30
Semi-Pelagianism, 88
sensus plenior, 11
simile, 53
sin, 16
Slater, Jonathan, 113
sonship, 41, 54, 80, 90
Spear, Wayne, 120
Staniloae, Dumitru, 98
Starr, James, 96n33
Stedman, Rowland, 3, 51–52, 80–81,
  119–21
substitution, 60–61, 62–63, 64
suffering, 129–31
Suh, Chul Won, 41n75

Tertullian, 20
theōsis, 91–102, 107
theotokos, 23, 24–25, 27
Thirty-Nine Articles, 77
Thomas Aquinas, 101
Tipton, Lane, 85n1, 129, 134, 137
Torrance, Thomas F., 37, 76, 78
tree of the knowledge of good and evil,
  15
Trinity, 37–38, 48–49
  in creation, 11
  and Lord's Supper, 126
  and resurrection, 136
tritheism, 64n13

union with Christ
  and atonement, 60–65
  and creation, 18
  in death, 132–34
  and election, 65–72
  and incarnation, 40–43
  and justification, 5–6, 77
  in Leontius of Jerusalem, 31–32
  and *ordo salutis*, 88–91
  in Reformed theology, 102–23
  and resurrection, 6–7, 134–38
  and sanctification, 6
  as substantial, 105–6, 114, 117–18, 123
  and suffering, 129–31
  and transformation, 85–87, 102–28

Vermigli, Pietro Martire, 108–9
virgin birth, 20
Vos, Geerhardus, 89, 90n8

Watts, Isaac, 90
weight of glory, 131
Wenham, Gordon, 11
Western church, 100
Westminster Assembly, 2, 64, 71, 90
Westminster Confession of Faith, 71–72,
  74–76, 120
Westminster Larger Catechism, 76–78,
  141
Williams, Anna, 101
will of God, as one, 64n13
Word and sacraments, 124–25
Wordworth, Christopher, 40
wrath of God, 62, 74, 83
Wright, N. T., 6n16

Zanchius, Hieronymous, 67–69, 71, 72,
  79
Zwinglianism, 120–21